Lifeviews

BY R. C. Sproul:

Lifeviews

R.C. SPROUL

Fleming H. Revell
Old Tappan, New Jersey

TO: Dr. Thomas Gregory: teacher, counselor, friend.

Library of Congress Cataloging in Publication Data

Sproul, R. C. (Robert Charles), 1939–
  Lifeviews.

  Includes index.
  1. Apologetics—20th century. 2. Christianity and
culture. 3. Ideology. I. Title. II. Title: Life
views
BT1102.S588 1986   261   85-28282
ISBN 0-8007-5357-7

Publisher's Foreword

IN A WORLD THAT HAS BECOME AN INTERRELATED GLOBAL VILLAGE of 4.5 billion men, women, and children, the problems of human existence have reached crisis proportions. Modern man stretches to achieve new heights, but his very advances in technological and scientific realms sometimes threaten him with the loss of life's most precious gifts—and even life itself. In the midst of the crises, Christians believe the possibility for unprecedented good, for the flourishing of freedom, and for peace exists. This hopeful outlook is itself possible in a violent, threatened world because the Christian views the world from the center point of history, the Cross, where God dealt redemptively with the crux of the human problem.

While the Christian does not doubt God's ability nor His final victory, he struggles to know and to implement God's plan. Thankfully, there is an ongoing discussion of contemporary problems as Christians wrestle with agendas for action. As the publisher of the Crucial Questions series, we earnestly hope that these volumes will contribute positively to that discussion. Although the viewpoints expressed by the authors in this series may not always be those of the publisher, we are grateful for the opportunity to present them to the public, and we trust that these volumes will serve to stimulate Christians to fulfill their role as salt and light in today's world.

94430

Contents

Preface

PHILOSOPHY IS a difficult science. It is the goal of this book to try and make the difficult more simple. This book is a layman's guide to understanding complex strands of ideas that shape our culture.

I have tried to paint with a broad brush, avoiding technical matters as much as possible. The book is designed not only for individual use but for group discussions, and is to be a stimulus for further thinking, reading, and discussion.

Special thanks are in order for Lynda McIntyre for typing the manuscript and to Fleming H. Revell Publishers for having the vision to seek simplified tools for helping people understand the world they live in.

Part I
World Views

Chapter One

The Importance of Cultural Awareness

EVERY CHRISTIAN IS a missionary. If we carefully read the book of Acts, we will see that when persecution arose in Jerusalem, all the Christians were scattered except the apostles. Those who were scattered abroad went everywhere preaching the Gospel (Acts 8). That was the way the Christian church multiplied. It was not by an ordained clergy, by the apostles, or even by the deacons. It was the rank and file of Christians who took the Gospel wherever they went in the ancient world. In other words, they were missionaries.

In the modern church we make a distinction between the "professional missionary" and the "layman." The distinction is between paid missionaries and volunteers, between "full-time" hired employees and rank-and-file church members. Sadly, it has come to mean that the paid professionals are responsible to do the missions task. The layperson's job is to pray for the missionary, give tithes to the missionary, and in other ways encourage the missionary. The missionaries are the players; the rest of us are cheerleaders.

God teaches us otherwise. Of course there is a special place for the paid professional. However, the biblical definition of a missionary has nothing to do with salary. A missionary is not simply "one who is paid." In biblical terms a missionary is "one who is *sent.*" Here is the crux of the matter. We are all sent. It is our calling to be witnesses. Every Christian must get in the game. There are no cheerleaders—only players.

Some missionaries go to Africa—others travel to the Orient or to Europe. Every missionary goes somewhere. We all have a mission field, if only our own neighborhood or office building. Every corner of the world is a mission field. There are no boundaries in this world beyond which Christian witness is out of bounds.

Suppose for a moment that you had the opportunity to meet Jesus face to face. If in that meeting you had the chance to ask Jesus one question, what would you ask Him? The disciples had the opportunity to ask Jesus questions every day. They asked Him how to pray, how to heal the sick, and questions about theology. There came a moment, however, when they were down to their last question. They stood with Jesus on the Mount of Olives, the mountain of ascension. Jesus was about to depart from them. The cloud of Shekinah glory was ready to envelop Christ and lift Him to heaven. Jesus was leaving this planet.

There was time for one more question. What was it? The disciples asked, "Lord, are you at this time going to restore the kingdom to Israel?" (Acts 1:6 NIV). I wonder why they asked that question. Wouldn't it be nice if Jesus had answered, "Yes. The work is finished. I am going to the right hand of the Father. As soon as I arrive and am enthroned as King of Kings and Lord of Lords you can all enjoy a vacation. I'll take care of everything. I'll make sure that every element of the world recognizes My reign. We will make an official announcement by writing it in the sky. Then I will send angels to every remote part of the globe to make absolutely certain that everybody knows that I am now the king of the universe. You fellows take a rest. Go back up in the stands and enjoy the game."

We know that is not what Jesus said. Rather He answered their question something like this: "Look, it's none of your business *when* the kingdom is going to be restored to Israel. My Father has a timetable for that. What *is* your business is *Be My witnesses*."

The kingdom of God is real. At this very moment Jesus sits in the seat of cosmic authority. He is now the supreme ruler of the world. He stands over the governments of this world. He is King. The Premier of the Soviet Union must answer to Him. The Dalai Lama of Tibet must answer to Him. The Prince of Morocco must answer to Him. The President of the United States must answer to Him. But there is one big problem. His kingdom is *invisible*. Not everyone knows about it. All over the world people are living as if Jesus were not King.

Some people believe that there is no God. Others say that there are many gods. Some folks believe that man is supreme. Others believe that man is worthless. Many people believe there is a God, but they live as if there were no God. Still others ask, "What difference does it make?"

Where Christ is invisible, people perish. Where His reign is unknown or ignored, people are exploited. They are demeaned. They are enslaved. They are butchered. They are aborted. They are raped. They are casualties of war. They are robbed. They are slandered. They are oppressed. They are cheated in marriage. They are cheated in their wages. They are left to go hungry, naked, and unsheltered. They are consigned to loneliness. They are ridiculed. They are frightened—that and a whole lot more, is what difference it makes.

We Are All Missionaries

In all of life's situations we are to be His witnesses. Our job is to *make the invisible reign of Jesus visible.* The world is shrouded in darkness. Nothing is visible in the dark. No wonder then that we are called to be the light of the world. Every single one of us has a mission. We have all been sent to bear witness to Christ. That means simply that we are all missionaries.

Imagine being sent to a foreign country as a missionary without any prior training. Imagine receiving no instructions about who the people are, what language they speak, or how they think. Before a missionary can go to a foreign field, that person must study the country in depth. He must learn the language and the customs and gain some insight into how the people think. A tribe in the jungle has a vastly different outlook contrasted to middle-class suburbanites or inner-city apartment dwellers.

Let's assume that we are missionaries to the United States. What is needed for our preparation? It's not enough simply to know the content of the Gospel. It is also important that we understand the society in which we are acting out our role as missionaries. Helping you to understand our culture is the purpose of this book. It is an attempt to describe the culture of the United States as it now exists, to show how this culture affects Christians, and to suggest how we can respond biblically to that culture as Christian witnesses.

It would be a dreadful mistake for us to assume that our culture is a predominantly Christian one. Yet our country doesn't deserve the term "pagan" either. Our country has been strongly influenced by Christianity and by Christian values. Some have suggested that we have been influenced in the same way people are "influenced" when they receive an inoculation to prevent a disease. They are given a small dose of the disease, just enough of it to be immune to the real thing. Perhaps that is what has happened in our American culture: just enough Christianity has penetrated our society to make us "immune" to the Gospel.

Our nation is not pagan, because paganism is a pre-Christian condition that exists where the Gospel has never been preached. That is not the case in the United States. Ours is what I call a secular environment, a secular society. The secularization of the American society is a *post-Christian* phenomenon, not a pre-Christian one. Pre-Christian is pagan. Post-Christian is secularized.

It is also important to understand that our culture is a melting pot. We do not live in a culture that is uniform, where only a single definable world view or value system is operating. In China, for example, we find a uniform system of thought that everyone is required to embrace. It is taught in the schools and advertised on posters. The uniformity even comes down to people dressing in the same way—literally in uniforms. The costume of the premier is basically the same as that of the peasant.

Such uniformity has not been the American experience. We have been a melting pot of people and, therefore, of ideas. The result has been that many different beliefs and philosophies compete for acceptance within our society. We are not uniform but pluralistic. The melting pot metaphor is perhaps misleading because we have a pot where everything goes in but everything doesn't mix. There is an overarching national culture with many distinctive subcultures, in New York City, in Hollywood, in the Midwest, and so on. There are also socioeconomic classes and many of them have distinctive values. One categorization shows nine such classes: lower-lower, middle-lower, upper-lower, lower-middle, middle-middle, upper-middle, lower-upper, middle-upper, and upper-upper. If we as Christian missionaries are to be able to communicate to this diverse society, we need to be aware of the dominant systems of thought that are at work within our society.

To understand a melting pot culture is not easy. Things get mixed up in a melting pot. When conflicting ideas are stirred up it tends to get confusing. We may be able to identify the particular subculture we live in or the socioeconomic group to which we belong, but that is not enough to identify our values. We are all thrown in the pot. We are exposed to or influenced by a wide diversity of ideas. We get one set of ideas in church. Another in school. We learn one set of values watching "Dallas" or "Dynasty" and another from watching "Little House on the Prairie." We observe one philosophy at the Democratic National Convention and another at the Republican National Convention. One view of life is evident in *Chariots of Fire* and another in *Scarface*. Johnny Cash sings one kind of song, Prince another. Norman Rockwell represents one kind of portrait, Andy Warhol another.

All these perspectives bombard our brains and shape our thinking. The diversity and confusion are so great that for most of us it seems that the melting pot is found not so much in the culture but in our own hands and that the asparagus is getting stuck to the pasta. The result is a basic inconsistency in our lives, an inconsistency we are often unaware of. We respond. We react. We feel. But we are not always sure why we respond the way we do.

If it is difficult for us to understand our own culture, imagine the horrors an alien would experience in trying to sort it out. Imagine a real life extraterrestial visiting our nation and trying to understand our behavior at the Stock Exchange or the Super Bowl. It would be something like the Martian who was ordered to observe our sporting games and report back to his superior. When his mission was accomplished he turned in his report about football, baseball, basketball, hockey, boxing, car racing, and others. Then he mentioned the strangest game of all. It was a game men played with sticks and a little white ball. His superior asked the name of the game. The Martian replied, "I think it's called, 'Oh, *#@!' " He explained that men took clubs and swung at this little ball and after each swing declared, "Oh, *#@!"

The confusion of ideas and viewpoints became a national crisis when the Supreme Court ruled on the volatile issue of prayer in the public schools. The basic principle in view was that a religious view of life should not be imposed on the people by the state in a public schoolroom. The problem was that the only option to a religious viewpoint was a nonreligious viewpoint. If the state propagates a religious viewpoint the nonreligious people feel discriminated against. If the state propagates a nonreligous viewpoint then the religious people feel discriminated against.

The solution to the crisis was formulated in the concept of a "neutral" education. A neutral education is one that is neither proreligion or antireligion. It is neither pro-God nor anti-God. It seeks to keep God out of educational issues. The only problem with the solution is that the ideal is impossible. There is no such thing as a neutral education. Every education, every curriculum has a viewpoint. That viewpoint either considers God in it or it does not. To teach children about life and the world in which they live without reference to God is to make a statement about God. It screams a statement. The message is either that there is no God or that God is irrelevant. Either way the message is the same—there is no God. An irrelevant God is the same as no God at all. If God is, then He must be relevant—to His entire creation.

The pastor of a local congregation announced good news to his people. The church was experiencing rapid growth and the church building was now too small to accommodate them. The church was located in an area where property was selling at premium prices, costing about $100,000 an acre. The building committee had tried desperately to find acreage at an affordable price, but there was no land available near the church. Time after time they had approached landowners but none was willing to sell. The pastor told the story:

> I have good news. As you know, we have prayed that God would open doors for us. We decided to approach a particular landowner one last time who has repeatedly turned us down. When we went to him he had just experienced an unexpected turn of events with a parcel of ground. He agreed to sell it to us *and* to donate four hundred thousand dollars of the purchase price!

The pastor said it was an answer to prayer. Was it? He said that God had opened the door for the property. Had He? What happened here? Was this a case of divine providence at work or was it merely the mortal machinations of a business deal? If there is no God then the answer is easy—it was a sheer human deal and any appeal to Providence is a delusion. If there is a God who answers prayers then the pastor was correct in calling his congregation to a spirit of gratitude before God.

How we understand the incident depends on how we view the world we live in. It depends on whether we think God is sovereign over life or if we think nobody is home in heaven.

Christians or Pragmatists?

Most of us are inconsistent about such matters. Our viewpoint comes from the melting pot. We get mixed up. Our pot has a dash of faith and a dash of skepticism. We are at once religious and secular. We believe in God, sometimes. Our religion has elements of superstition at some times and is tempered by sober science at other times. We are at the same time Christians and card-carrying pragmatists. On Sunday we say the creed. On Monday we are fatalists. We try to separate our religious life from the rest of our life. We live by holding contradictory beliefs. Living in contradictions can be exciting. Life is surely more than logic. But the contradictory life is a confusing life, a life of inconsistency and incoherence. Its bottom line is chaos.

We are inconsistent and confused because we fail to understand where Christianity ends and paganism begins. We do not know where the boundary lines are. Consequently we traffic back and forth across the lines, making forays between darkness and light. We are lost in our own culture, swirling around in the melting pot while somebody else has his hand on the spoon. We're not sure whether we are the witnesses or the ones being witnessed to. We don't know if we are the missionaries or the mission field.

It was Socrates who said that the unexamined life is not worth living. To examine one's life is to think about it. It is to *evaluate*. To evaluate requires examining values and value systems. We all have values. We all have some viewpoint about what life is all about. We all have some perspective on the world we live in. We are not all philosophers but we all have a philosophy. Perhaps we haven't thought much about that philosophy, but one thing is certain—we live it out. How we live reveals our deepest convictions about life.

Our lives say much more about how we think than our books do. The theories we preach are not always the ones we actually believe. The theories we live are the ones we really believe.

I once heard a sermon entitled "Christians, Think!" The exhortation contained the repeated refrain, "Christians, Think!" The comma is crucial. The preacher was not telling us that Christians are people who think. He was summoning us to be Christians who do think. The purpose of this book is to help us think about prevailing viewpoints in our culture.

We will be examining perspectives on life in the chapters that follow. These perspectives are existentialism, humanism, pragmatism, positivism, pluralism (and its corollary, relativism) and hedonism. All are, to varying degrees, affecting the way Americans think and act today. As Christians we are being bombarded daily by the influences of these philosophies. I doubt if there has been a period in all of Christian history when *so many Christians* are *so ineffectual* in shaping the culture in which they live as is true right now in the United States. Perhaps it is because we are intimidated and overwhelmed by the onslaught of these different philosophical systems. Combating this onslaught is a major challenge facing Christians today.

Questions for Discussion

1. Where can you function as a missionary?

2. How many subcultural groups do you belong to?

3. Who is doing the outreach ministry in your church?

4. Why is the kingdom of God invisible?

5. How much authority does Jesus have right now?

6. What does it mean to be a "witness" to Christ?

7. What is the difference between paganism and secularism?

8. Who influences your values?

9. How did your education deal with the relationship of God to the world?

10. How relevant is God to the nightly news?

Chapter Two

Secularism: Ignoring the Eternal

STUDENTS OF HISTORY realize that no society can survive, no civilization can function, without some unifying system of thought. All societies are made up of different people, different jobs, different values, and different classes. In a broad sense, all societies are melting pots.

How do the parts fit together to make a whole? What makes a society a unified system? Some kind of glue is required in order for the parts to stick together. The glue is found in a unifying system of thought, what we call a "world view." Various world views can spring from diverse sources. The world view can be built upon a philosophy system such as Platonism or on a religion as in the case of Old Testament Israel. Other civilizations have been unified by a common mythology. Still others came together by a devotion to the state and a particular political philosophy.

Yet in all societies we find elements of philosophy, religion, mythology, and politics, all competing for the rank of dominance. One of these elements will inevitably emerge as the dominant view to order and unify the society.

What dominates American culture? Is it religion? Is it philosophy? Is it mythology? Is it statism? I am sure we will hear voices from each of these claiming theirs as the dominant system. It is difficult to isolate America's dominant world view precisely because our culture is so diverse. We have an unusually free and open society where the battle of ideas takes place.

If there is a consensus among analysts of American culture they would agree that our unity is no longer (if ever) based on a religious system. Nor is mythology a likely candidate. Though we live in society with an ever-accelerating growth of central government we are not (yet) totally statist. That leaves one option, philosophy. But which philosophy? Is our world view found mainly in humanism? Pragmatism? Existentialism? Positivism?

Each of these schools of thought, as well as others, is flourishing in our day. They compete with each other. They coexist, not always peacefully, and make for strange bedfellows. The question that is provoked is one of common denominator. Is there one dominant philosophy that can *include* these other schools as subheadings? Is there an *umbrella world view* that is broad enough to cover these other systems?

We believe that one current *ism* has emerged as the dominant world view of our culture. Before we explore it, however, it is important to understand the anatomy of an *ism*.

Ism is a suffix added to the root of a word. These three letters, when added to a root word, change the meaning of the term dramatically. It is one thing to be social, quite another to embrace socialism. It is one thing to be human, something else to adopt humanism. See, for example, how the following words are changed merely by adding the suffix *ism*.

national	national*ism*
impression	impression*ism*
feminine	femin*ism*
exhibition	exhibition*ism*
natural	natural*ism*
behavior	behavior*ism*
military	militar*ism*
moral	moral*ism*
peace	pacif*ism*
plural	plural*ism*
liberal	liberal*ism*

The list could go on. As soon as we put the suffix on the word it changes the word into a system of thought, a way of looking at things, a world view. Philosophers use the German word *Weltanschauung* to describe it. A *Weltanschauung* is a systematic way of looking at the world. It conditions how we interpret the meaning of daily life.

Again, we do not all look at things the same way. We all exist, but are not all existentialists. We are all thinking subjects but we do not all embrace subjectivism. We all have relatives but are not all relativists.

When Melville's Captain Ahab set out on his maniacal quest for the great white whale, Moby Dick, he tacked a gold doubloon to the mainmast and promised it as a reward for the first sailor to spot Moby Dick. As the sailors passed the gleaming coin they contemplated its meaning to them. One saw it as a symbol of great seamanship, another for how many cigars it would buy. The half-wit cabin boy, Pip, declared, "I see, you see, we all see." In his simple-mindedness Pip understood that everyone on board viewed the gold coin in a different way. How the sailors viewed life, how they viewed the world, determined how they viewed things in the world, including the gold coin.

The dominant ism of American culture, the ism reflected

in the news media, the film industry, the novel, and the art world is *secularism*. Secularism is the umbrella that shields the various competing philosophies beneath it. Secularism has the necessary common denominator to tie together humanism, pragmatism, relativism, naturalism, pluralism, existentialism, and several other isms.

What then, is secularism? What gives it the glue necessary to unify the other isms? To understand secularism as an ism we must first look at its root, *secular*, before we can see what magic is performed upon it by the addition of the suffix *ism*.

A Secular Priesthood

Historically, the word *secular* is a positive word in the Christian's vocabulary. The church has always had a good view of that which was regarded as secular. In the Middle Ages, for example, men were ordained to a specific role in the priesthood that was called the "secular priesthood." These were men who had responsibilities which took them out of the institution of the church to minister in the world where there were specific needs requiring the healing touch or the priestly mission of the church.

There is a sense of which I was ordained as a secular clergyman because I was ordained to the teaching ministry, not to an ecclesiastical office within a local congregation. I was commissioned to go to the university and become a teacher in the secular world. It is this secular world that can be distinguished, to some degree, from that sphere we have set apart and called the church, or the sacred realm. Often, in the minds of many Christians, the distinction between sacred and secular is the distinction between the good and the bad, but that is not the way it has been used in church history. Secular was simply a different sphere of operation.

The word *secular* has its origins and its roots in the Latin language and comes from the word *saeculum* which means "world." The secular priest is one who ministers in the world.

There is another Latin word for "world," *mundus*. One notable place it is used is on the tombstone of Athanasius, a fourth-century bishop who was a leading defender of the faith. His tombstone read, *Athanasius contra mundum*—"Athanasius against the world." If both words, *saeculum* and *mundus*, mean "world," what is the difference?

The people in the ancient world understood that, as human beings, they lived in time and space. We still talk that way. Our life is spatial, geographical. There is a certain "whereness" to our lives. We live within a time frame. Jesus talked about "this age," the present age. So in Latin the word for this world, in terms of time is *saeculum*. The word for this world, in terms of space, is *mundus*.

The secular refers then to this world in this time. Its point of focus is *here and now*. The accent of the secular is on the present time rather than on eternity. I live right now. I can look at the clock and watch the second hand move. I can hear it ticking.

Try a little experiment. Look at your wristwatch, if it has a second hand, or at a clock. Watch the entire face of the clock. Now wait until the second hand reaches 12. Look quickly at the 6. Watch the second hand sweep toward the 6. The 6 is still future as the second hand approaches it. What happens when the second hand reaches 6? Does it stop? No, unless your clock breaks. Now the 6 is past. It's over, gone forever. That part of your life is gone in an instant. We have just experienced time as it passes us by.

The question we ask is this: Is that all there is? Is there only time? This time? This secular moment? Or is there something else? Is there eternity beyond this world and this time? What we are really asking is, is there a God beyond this world who has always existed and will always exist? Does my personal life extend beyond the limits of this world?

We could ask the question another way. We start with the easy one. *Where* are you right now as you read these words? Can you identify your location? Are you in Chicago or San Francisco? What are you doing this moment? (I trust that you are reading.)

Those questions are easy. Let's make them a little more difficult. Where will you be tomorrow at exactly the same time? What time is it now? Add twenty-four hours and guess where you will be and what you will be doing. It has to be a guess, doesn't it? You don't know for sure because you can't possibly know for sure. You may have plans for tomorrow. You may even have a specific activity marked on your calendar for this specific time. The odds may favor that your guess will be correct. But you don't know for sure because you don't know that you will be alive at this time tomorrow or that the place you intend to be will still be there tomorrow.

These are the limits of being time-bound creatures. We guess about tomorrow; we hope for tomorrow; but tomorrow is always shrouded a bit in mystery for us. That is because we are secular. We live in a world of time.

Let's make the experiment even more difficult. Now note the time, the day, the month, and the year you are reading these words. Write them down. Now add one hundred years. Five hundred years. Where will you be one hundred years from now? Five hundred years? What will you be doing then?

Some of you are smiling. You're perhaps thinking, "Hey, that's not so difficult. I'll be in the boneyard somewhere pushing up daisies. I'll be fertilizer for the cemetery or part of the ingredients of 'Soylent Green.' " Perhaps you'll say,

"I'll be dead, but some of my genes will still be around in my great-grandchildren."

Secularism Versus Christianity

This is precisely where Christianity and secularism collide. This is the point of conflict. The biblical world view has a long-term view of human life. The term is much longer than that of secularism.

For secularism, all life, every human value, every human activity must be understood in light of this present time. The secularist either flatly denies or remains utterly skeptical about the eternal. He either says there is no eternal or if there is we can know nothing about it. What matters is *now* and only *now*. All access to the above and the beyond is *blocked*. There is no exit from the confines of this present world. The secular is all that we have. We must make our decisions, live our lives, make our plans, all within the closed arena of this time—the here and now.

That obviously brings conflict with Christianity. In the New Testament the biblical world view is always concerned with the long-term. The Bible teaches us that we are created for eternity. The heart of the New Testament message is that Christ has come to give us a life that wells up into eternal life. The startling news is that we will get out of this world alive.

The biblical starting point for understanding the world is found on page one of Genesis. We read, "In the beginning God created the heaven and the earth" (Genesis 1:1). We look at the earth and we see that it has a beginning in space and time. But before there was even a world, there is One who transcends the world, One who is outside of the restrictions of this space and time order that we call the world—namely God. "In the beginning, God." At the core of our Christian faith, we believe in a God who is beyond the confines of this planet and who is eternal. All judgments that God makes, all things that He does, are done from the perspective of the eternal.

In philosophy, we say that God considers everything *sub specie aeternitatis*. That is merely a fancy Latin phrase meaning that God considers everything "under the species" or auspices, or from the perspective of, the eternal. The admonition and rebuke that Christ brings to this world is that men are only thinking of the short-term. They are thinking of the now and only the now, instead of the long-term consequences of their behavior. Jesus says that He comes from above. He descends from the eternal realm. He calls the Christian to live his life in light of eternity. A Christian's values are to be measured by transcendent norms of eternal significance.

I write a column in *Table Talk*, the magazine of Ligonier Ministries, and I call it "Right Now Counts Forever." I chose that title for a reason. If there is one message that I can give to my generation it is this: Right now counts forever. What you and I do now has eternal significance. The now is important because it counts for a long, long time. The secular is important because it is linked forever to the sacred.

When I chose that title I was acutely aware that we, as Christians, are being pressed on every side by the philosophy of the secularist. The secularist declares, "Right now counts for . . . right now!" There is no eternity, there is no eternal perspective. There are no absolutes. There are no abiding principles by which human life is to be judged, embraced, or evaluated. All reality is restricted or limited to the now.

We see this view in different forms in theology. We have seen an attempt in the twentieth-century theology to produce a secularized gospel. Remember the "Death of God" movement? One of the most important books that came out of that movement was called *The Secular Meaning of the Gospel* by Dr. Paul Van Buren. Van Buren talked of synthesizing classical Christianity with the philosophy of secularism. That simply cannot be done without first declaring the death of God. Secularism as an ism must include within its world view at least an implicit atheism.

The death of God, in terms of the loss of transcendence and the loss of the eternal, also means for us the death of man. It means that history has no transcendent goal. There is no eternal purpose. The meaning of our lives is summed up by the ciphers on our tombstone: "Born 1925, died 1985." We live between two points on a calendar. We have a beginning and an ending, with no ultimate significance.

We need not go to a library and take down a dusty tome of philosophy to be exposed to the world view of secularism. The media screams it. We think, for example, of the beer commercial that says, "You only go around once in life, so grab for all the gusto you can get." We see a man on a sailboat, the wind blowing his hair and the salt spray splashing in his face. He's having a fantastic time *right now.* Pepsi calls ours "The Now Generation." "Do it now!" "Get it now!" The message that comes through is, "You'd better get it now because there is no tomorrow ultimately." Life is to be consumed in the present. Our philosophy must be a philosophy of the immediate.

The secularists of Jesus' day summed up their philosophy like this: "Eat, drink, and be merry. For tomorrow you die." Contrast that with Jesus' words: "Lay up for yourselves treasures in heaven." Think in terms of eternity. Think of the long-range implications. This touches us most directly, not simply in how we handle our bank accounts, but at the level of how we invest our lives. Life is an investment and the question that modern man has to answer is, "Am I going to invest my life for short-term benefits or for long-term gains?" Every time we are faced with a moral decision, with the temptation to do something now that may have harmful aftereffects, we are caught in the tension between two world views.

We cannot escape the secular. The world is our dwelling place. At times, Christians have sought to escape this world, to abandon it as an ungodly place. But where do we go? If we flee to the desert we have not left the world. Even monasteries have clocks. Our task is not to escape the secular, but secular*ism*. We must embrace the world without embracing worldliness.

The theologians who have sought to combine Christianity and secularism are on a fool's errand. It cannot be done. The root concepts of Christianity cannot be unified with the root concepts of secularism. If we seek to breed them the result will be a grotesque hybrid. It will be sterile, like a mule, powerless to reproduce. If we seek to effect a synthesis between two radically conflicting world views, we must inevitably submerge one into the other. The result of such bastardization can be neither Christianity nor secularism. If a Christian buys into secularism his world view is no longer Christian. If a secularist buys into Christianity he is no longer a secularist.

It was Aristotle who said that in the mind of every wise man resides the corner of a fool. Perhaps the reverse is also true. Perhaps inside the head of every fool resides the corner of the wise man. In biblical terms foolishness is deemed a moral act as well as an intellectual one. It involves more than mental error; it is also wicked. We are not to suffer fools gladly. Yet there are times we can learn something even from the fool.

What, apart from wickedness, could ever motivate someone to seek an unholy alliance between Christianity and secularism? Is any good motivation to be found there? I think there is. The secularist reacts negatively to religious people who are "so heavenly minded that they are of no earthly good." He reacts against a kind of distorted religious faith that neglects the vital concerns of this world. He rejects a reservation mentality where Christians isolate themselves from the pain and struggles of this world. Many professing Christians have "dropped out," preferring to look to the future world alone. They embrace a spurious spirituality, which gives license for neglecting this world.

We Are Called to Be Secular People

Such a standpoint cannot be found in the New Testament. The Christ of Scripture was profoundly concerned with this world. This world was the site and purpose of the Incarnation. The God of heaven so loved this world that He sent His Son to redeem it. This is the world God created. This is the world God is redeeming. There is no other theater of God's redemptive action than this world. There is a profound sense in which we are called to be secular people.

When Harvey Cox wrote *The Secular City*, it was clear that one of his grand passions was that the church be "where the action is." On this point he was echoing the plea of Martin Luther that the church be "profane." What Luther meant by a profane church was not that the church should indulge in uttering obscenities or use gutter language. Rather, Luther was playing with the Latin roots for the word *profane*. Profane originally meant simply "outside of the temple." In Luther's terms a profane church is one that moves out of the temple and into the world.

There is a tendency for Christians to seek shelter in the temple. The disciples wanted to stay on the mount of transfiguration. At the death of Jesus they huddled in the upper room with the doors shut because they feared the Jews. Jesus sent them down from the mountain of transfiguration. He virtually broke down the door of the upper room to send them to the uttermost corners of the earth. Our Lord had no time for isolationism. He had an agenda for the world.

Luther also argued that a mature Christian must be secular in the sense that he must embrace the world. He detected a normal pattern in a growing Christian. The pattern begins with conversion, often followed by a sense of withdrawal from and rejection of this world. This period of retreat is marked by preoccupation with spiritual matters. But at the point of maturity there must be a kind of re-entry into the world. This is not a return to worldliness. It is not a fall into secularism. It is a new appreciation of the world as the theater of redemption. It is recognizing that this is our Father's world and not a place to be despised or ignored.

The Christian must *distinguish* between the secular and the sacred, but never *separate* them. To separate them is to deny the agenda of Christ. The voices of the theologians who go too far in embracing secularism serve as a warning to us. They don't separate the secular and the sacred; they confuse them. They stress the now and neglect the eternal. We must guard against stressing the eternal so much that we neglect the now. A Christian world view must be concerned with the temporal and the eternal. There must be no false dichotomy between the two.

At the core of our moral behavior are actions. Every action not only has a cause, but also a result. Results, or consequences, take us to tomorrow and beyond. What did Macbeth say? "Tomorrow, and tomorrow, and tomorrow, creeps in this petty pace from day to day, To the last syllable of recorded time." But for the Christian, there is no "last syllable of recorded time." Our lives are forever. Beyond the secular or *saeculum* there is the eternal. That is what the Christian faith is all about.

Why should a person be worried about salvation in terms of personal redemption if there is no eternal dimension? What is the mission of the church if secularism is correct? Why should we be concerned about the redemption of individuals if there is no tomorrow? All we can really do is minimize pain and suffering for a season. The secularist can never offer ultimate answers to the human predicament because, for him, there are no ultimate answers—because there is no ultimate realm. This side of eternity is the exclusive sphere of human activity. It is not by accident, as we will see, that most of those who accept secularism and who are thinking people, ultimately embrace a philosophy of despair. That despair will manifest itself in escapism through drugs, alcohol, and other forms of behavior that dull the senses from the message that is being proclaimed, indeed screamed, from every corner of our culture: "There is no tomorrow ultimately." It is a philosophy of despair and it is right now competing for people's minds in the United States.

In the chapters to follow, we will be looking at the elements that make up secularism: secularistic existentialism, secular humanism, and positivism. Although these different philosophies may seem to be on a collision course with each other, they all embrace one common point, namely, the denial of the transcendent and the eternal. Look for it in your culture. Be aware of it when you see it. We need to understand this world and this society in which we live.

The diagram below illustrates our cultural situation:

ETERNAL REALM

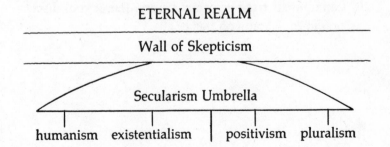

Questions for Discussion

1. What philosophies are you aware of in your culture?

2. What is the common denominator of secularistic philosophies?

3. What is the ultimate goal of your life?

4. Do you believe in life after death?

5. Do you believe there is ultimate justice?

6. What is your attitude toward the world?

7. Do you ever feel trapped by the pressures of the immediate?

8. What difference does it make if there is no God?

9. Why is it impossible to marry Christianity and secularism?

10. Can ultimate truth be contradictory? (Limit your discussion to four hours on this one!)

Chapter Three

Pessimistic Existentialism

"MAN IS A USELESS PASSION." These words penned by the French philosopher Jean-Paul Sartre provide the model of modern existentialism. In this simple statement are found the most basic elements of a modern theory of man. It is a bottom-line judgment, a grim conclusion to the question, "What's it all about?"

In its most basic definition existentialism is a philosophy about human existence. It views man not so much in terms of his mind or his soul, but of his will, his feelings. Man is a creature of passion. He feels strongly. He cares about life. He cries, he sings, he yearns, he curses. Human life cannot be reduced to elementary structures of biology. Man cannot be understood simply by his intellectual activity. It is his passion that makes him a man.

In former days when we wanted to know a person's views on a particular topic, we would pose the question like this: "What do you *think* about that?" Now the question is usually stated differently: "What do you *feel* about that?" The accent has changed from thinking to feeling. Feelings have become the new standard of human "truth." Even our ethics are decided by the litmus test of passion. Our moral creed is "If it feels good, it is good." Or, to state it in musical terms that light up our lives, "It can't be wrong when it feels so right."

To test objective truth by subjective feelings seems at first glance as a rather bizarre way of going about things. But think (or feel) about it for a moment. If man is a passion, then his passion must be his most important standard. A man lives every moment with his feelings. We respond to life from a feeling level. Our guts lead our minds more often than our minds lead our guts.

Sartre was not suggesting that man no longer has a mind or that man never thinks. He knew better than that. Rather, it is a matter of accent. Paul Tillich spoke of God in terms of "Ultimate Concern." Concern or caring is central to an existential view of the world.

To understand the philosophy of existentialism we must know a little bit of its background and what provoked it. In the past some philosophers were fond of creating massive systems or theories about man and his world. The goal was to achieve an *objective* view of the *essence* of humanness. Man sought to stand aloof from his own concerns to reflect on who he is. But there is something terribly dry and dull about the concept of humanness. What is humanness? Are you a humanness?

Even if we consider a more common term such as *humanity* we are left with the same problem. Humanity is a kind of "man-in-general." Does anybody want to be a "man-in-general"? We know men, particularly colonels, who want to be generals, but there are few who desire to be general men.

Words like *humanness, humanity,* or *man-in-general* are abstractions. They lack life. When we seek to define man in "objective terms" we often overlook the sense in which man is a subject. Even the very term *man* can provoke an allergic reaction. The reaction comes not only from women who are angry about being subsumed under the broader category of "man," but also from males who are existentialists. The protest of the existentialist is this: *There is no such thing as man, only men and women.*

The words *man* and *mankind* are what philosophers call "universals." Again, they are abstract concepts about a group or a class. When societies place the stress on groups or classes usually the individual person gets lost or eclipsed. In our society we speak, for example, of corporations as if they were living creatures. We say that corporations pay taxes. We sometimes forget that corporations are people. The personal element is obscured by abstract universals.

An abstract universal is an attempt to get at what we call the essence of a thing. We know that there are men. But why do we call men, "men"? There are only individuals, and each individual person is different from every other individual person. Yet there are similarities among individuals. Most of us have two arms and two legs, a nose, a mouth, and ears. But so do baboons. What happens if we lose a leg? Do we stop being men?

When we try to define a human being, we try to isolate the unique factors that make us human rather than baboons or daffodils. We are looking for the "essence" that makes us human rather than something else. What is this common essence that we share as human beings?

Plato wrestled with this problem in the ancient world. He sought for a definition of *man* that would set him apart from all other creatures. He thought he had discovered an acceptable definition when he called man a "featherless biped." The definition worked fine until one of Plato's enterprising students threw a plucked chicken over the wall with a sign attached to it that read, "Plato's man."

Existential philosophers are not satisfied with defining man as a plucked chicken. They are not fond of any definition of man that leaves us in the realm of abstract "essences." The axiom set forth by Sartre was that *existence precedes essence.* It is the existence of man (or more properly, "men") that matters, not some abstract essence.

Of course existential philosophers still speak of man-in-general. It is difficult to escape it altogether. Our opening quotation from Sartre bears witness to that. Remember the quote? "Man is a useless passion." Sartre did not say, "Men are useless passions." In this quotation Sartre began with essence rather than existence. But again, the accent, the point of concern is with concrete existence rather than with abstract essence.

There are different types of existential philosophers. We will examine later those who have tried to combine existential philosophy with Christianity in an optimistic way. Our concern for the moment, however, is with the pessimistic variety. Sartre does not rest with saying that man is a passion. He stresses the morbid conclusion that he is a *useless* passion. Here is the crux of pessimistic existentialism.

The term *useless* is ominous. It rivals its synonym *futile* for being one of the most terrifying words in the English language. That my passions should be useless or futile is to force me to despair. It is not by accident that the word *despair* is a much used term in existential literature.

Useless passions are passions that are futile. They have no meaning. Sartre's grim conclusion is that all of our caring, our concerns, our deepest aspirations are empty of significance. Human life is meaningless. It is a cosmic joke and the cold, impersonal, indifferent universe is the comedian. It would be better for us if the universe were hostile. At least we could be involved with an enemy that might possibly be vanquished or persuaded to be more friendly. But an indifferent universe is a universe that doesn't care. It doesn't care, because it cannot care; it is impersonal.

Is There Anyone Who Can Help?

Our dilemma is this: We are caring persons living in a world that doesn't care. We cannot look above the universe or outside the universe to find someone who cares. There is nobody out there; there is nobody home in heaven. Dr. James Montgomery Boice tells the story of an amateur mountain climber who fell over the side of a steep precipice which dropped off to a cavern thousands of feet below. One lone scraggly bush clung to the face of the cliff and the climber desperately grasped it to keep from plunging into the abyss. But the bush was not strong enough to bear his weight and began slowly to work lose from its roots. In sheer terror the climber screamed to heaven, "Is there anyone up there who can help me?" Suddenly a sonorous bass voice was heard from the clouds. "Yes, I can help you. But you must trust me. Let go of the bush." The climber stole a glance downward and then looked again toward heaven. He exclaimed, "Is there anyone *else* up there who can help?!"

The father of pessimistic existentialism was Friedrich Nietzsche, who was famous for penning the slogan "God is dead." Nietzsche took the philosophy of secularism to its logical conclusion. He understood that if this time is the only time, and this world is the only world, then there is no God. If there is no God, then life is meaningless. If all of human existence is shut up in the here and now, then all human values are arbitrary. If there is no exit to the eternal, then values and truth and ethics are a matter of pure decision. Right and wrong are simply what we have the courage to decide they are for ourselves.

Nietzsche made a distinction between what he called "herd morality" and "master morality." Herd morality is the morality practiced by the masses. It is based on the conventions of a society. People obey these societal rules and taboos like unthinking cattle. They go along with the herd, never asking penetrating questions about the rules of the game. They are like Americans who accept without criticism cultural contradictions. They never dare to tell the emperor that he has no clothes. They allow themselves to be ruled by the whims of the rulers. (Who, for example, dares to question the consistency of a graduated income tax in a society committed to the principle of justice for all? It is like affirming an equitable inequity.)

For Nietzsche the true existential man, the *authentic* man, creates his own morality. He refuses to follow the herd. He is his own master, a "Superman." He is the heroic sort who sails his ship into uncharted waters and builds his house on the slopes of Mount Vesuvius. He is defiant toward conventions. He dares the lava to flow down on his roof.

The Nietzschean hero is like a character in a Hemingway novel. He is the old man who challenges the sea, the soldier who ignores the tolling bell, the matador who grabs the bull by the horns, the man not intimidated by the slopes of Kilimanjaro. He is like Jimmy Cagney in *The White Cliffs of Dover*, who when his fighter plane was crippled by enemy gunfire, found he was headed directly toward the chalky cliffs. At the last second before impact Cagney spit at the cliff through the shattered windshield. The screen faded to black and the house lights came on while the audience was screaming wildly for their defiant hero.

There is a small problem here. After the theater emptied somebody began to think that on the morrow the sun would come up on the white cliffs of Dover. They would remain undaunted by the blemish left by the puny plane. The plane, meanwhile, was a twisted wreck at the bottom of the sea, a metal coffin for its dead pilot.

Nietzsche understood all that. Even his "master," his heroic Superman was destined to meaninglessness.

Nietzsche's brand of existential philosophy is called *nihilism*, which literally means "nothingness." If there is "nothing" out there, then nothing really matters. Life is the tale of the idiot, full of sound and fury, full of passion, signifying *nothing*. It is a useless passion; it is a futile fury.

Why Has Existentialism Spread So Rapidly?

Philosophical concepts usually take many years to "trickle down" from the scholars to the layman. It is usually a long and slow journey from the ivory tower to Main Street. A philosophical perspective set forth in abstract, academic writings will normally not attract popular attention or have much influence in a society until long after the originator is dead. In our lifetime, however, there has been a notable exception.

The rapid spread and enormous impact of existential philosophy upon our culture has been uncanny. I doubt if there has been any philosophical system that has had as much influence on American culture in the twentieth century as this school of thought. We encounter the influence of existentialism virtually every day of our lives and in virtually every sphere of our culture. Few people can define it or articulate its theory, but we are living under its influence every day.

Why has existentialism moved so rapidly from the theoretical level to the grass roots of our culture? First, it is because the chief advocates of existentialism have not only been brilliant technical philosophers, but they have also included some extraordinarily gifted men who have been able to translate their ideas into a more popular medium.

Notable among these was Sartre who, on the one hand, could produce a thick volume of weighty philosophy called *Being and Nothingness* and yet take those same heavy ideas and disperse them into the culture through the media of plays and novels.

Albert Camus, another Frenchman, was able to communicate his existential views through his essays and novels.
He was concerned with individual freedom and responsibility, with the alienation of the individual from society, and
with the difficulty of facing life without belief in God or
moral absolutes. He expressed his concerns in novels such
as *The Stranger*, *The Plague*, and *The Fall*, and in his play
Caligula.

A second reason existentialism has made its influence felt
is that the philosophy is itself, by definition, hostile to systems. It is an antisystem. It thrives not so much on an inter-
connected, coherent, well-related world view, as much as it
builds upon singular flashes of insight, brilliant vignettes
drawn from the close regions of daily life.

Ultimately existentialism has made its powerful presence
felt by abstract questions because it speaks directly to the
human predicament. Its emphasis, as the name implies, is
on human existence, on real, passionate life. Here we have a
philosophy that touches us where we live.

Existentialism made its impact felt most heavily in
America after World War II. Sartre and Camus had been
deeply involved in the war in Europe, working with the un-
derground resistance movement in France. When the atrocities that were associated with the holocaust in Western
Europe were exposed, a mood of despair enveloped the
continent. The philosophers looked at the atrocities of Bu-
chenwald, of Auschwitz, and elsewhere and said, "This is
what man is capable of doing." The spirit of optimism that
had characterized the nineteenth century was suddenly
plunged into despair.

Sartre's plays did much to communicate the motif and
mood of despair. He wrote one novel that bears the simple
title, *Nausea*. This was his evaluation of modern man. Sartre

argued that religious faith is irrational. It involves accepting what is "absurd."

Existential philosophy took root in artists' colonies, crossed the Atlantic and took up residence in the United States. One notable home was Greenwich Village, New York, with its "beatnik" movement and the "beat generation." The "beat generation" communicated some of the basic ideas of existentialism through art, poetry, literature, film, and theater. The arts have been major vehicles to communicate the ideas of existentialism to American society.

Theater of the Absurd

European films, such as those of Ingmar Bergman, Antonini, and Fellini have communicated some of the motifs of existentialism. The "theater of the absurd," a phenomenon that began in France in the 1950s and came to Broadway in the 1960s, was another vehicle of existentialism.

The theater of the absurd gained prominence with Samuel Beckett's play, *Waiting for Godot*. In this play, two vagrants pass the time while waiting for the unidentified Godot. But Godot never arrives. Godot is a thinly veiled characterization of God. The idea is that modern man lives in the absence of God. He waits for God, but God never shows up.

Beckett began writing in the early 1930s. His works portray man as an absurd and pathetic creature who lives in a meaningless, unintelligible universe. His best known novels include *Molloy, Malone Dies,* and *The Unnamable*.

The theater of the absurd went to such extremes that in some of the later productions, the actors would come out on the stage and utter unintelligible sounds over and over. They were saying (or more precisely, "babbling") that man has reached such a degree of irrationality that even human speech is no longer intelligible. There is no meaning to life. Meaning traditionally is communicated by words or by pictures that are easy to understand. The new message was: Life is meaningless. It is not a symphony; it's a cacophony. There is nothing that brings the universe together in a coherent fashion. Our universe is speeding away from rationality towards irrationality.

Religious movements also sprang up that embraced existential principles. Zen Buddhism was one such movement. It was the first significant penetration into Western culture from oriental religions. Zen is not pure Buddhism but an existential variety. In Zen, a person is to discipline his mind so that he can come into touch with his inner self. The person is to seek intuitive understanding of a larger "awareness." Yet this awareness yields the conclusion that life is irrational. It cannot be found in orderly systems. God is one hand clapping.

William Barrett has written an important study on existentialism which is one of the best introductions that I know of for the layman. It is not light reading nor is it simple, but it avoids the technical. It is titled *Irrational Man*, and I commend it to you. In it, Barrett makes this statement: "When mankind no longer lives spontaneously turned toward God or the super-sensible world—when, to echo the words of Yeats, The ladder is gone by which we would climb to a higher reality—the artist too must stand face to face with a flat and inexplicable world. This shows itself even in the formal structures of modern art. Where the movement of the spirit is no longer vertical but only horizontal, the climactic elements in art are in general leveled out, flattened."

What Barrett is saying is that the connection between earth and heaven has vanished. The vertical sphere, the upward dimension, is no longer the concern of the artist. Man is trapped in this horizontal dimension. (Does this sound familiar from our earlier discussion of secularism?)

One may see what appear to be bizarre forms of modern art. Consider cubism, for example. Look at Picasso's guitars with their strange shapes. See a face with three noses or three eyes. We may respond to such distortions by exclaiming, "That doesn't make sense to me." The artist would respond by saying, "That's because I'm compressing life and flattening it so that we understand that all of life must be understood on the horizontal level."

In the film industry the existentialist viewpoint brought a noticeable shift in plots and storylines. It used to be that the drama and the pathos of pain and death were followed by a happy ending. When I was a boy the Saturday afternoon matinees featured the likes of Roy Rogers or Gene Autry. I could always tell who the good guy was because he wore a white hat and he won in the end. He was noble, virtuous, and idealistic.

Hollywood picked up on the existentialist theme and began producing films of despair. The heroes began to wear black hats. A new era of realism was ushered in on Marlon Brando's motorcycle. The hero became an antihero. War was no longer glamorized. Vietnam had no place for John Wayne or Van Johnson. The Green Berets were no longer "Fighting Leathernecks." War was viewed in terms of *Catch-22* and *M*A*S*H*. The ultimate meaninglessness of life was communicated by Antonini's *Blow Up* and the Jane Fonda feature *They Shoot Horses, Don't They?*

The most obvious change in films came with respect to sex and violence. Here the passions of man were deromanticized. It was a long way from the "scandalous" suggested rape in *Duel in the Sun*, and the beach scene in *From Here to Eternity* to *Deep Throat* and *The Devil and Miss Jones*. Sex changed from an integral part of love to a base animal drive.

Graphic violence made an obvious transition from *The House of Frankenstein* to *Scarface*.

The film *Rocky* seemed like an anachronism. For a moment audiences breathed a sigh of relief as some good news came down. The old American dream was rekindled by the Italian Stallion whose dreams and aspirations did not end in despair. Adrianne's admonition, "Win, Rocky!" was a throwback to earlier days. The nostalgia went on with *Chariots of Fire*, a study in contrast to the normal Hollywood fare.

Another theme that appears frequently in existentialism is captured by the German word *Angst* (anxiety). Modern philosophers have done extensive investigation into the human feelings of anxiety. These are not specific anxieties such as a fear of flying or a fear of heights or of closed-in spaces. Those are traditional fears that have specifications attached to them. The *Angst* about which the philosopher speaks is an undefined, faceless, amorphous type of anxiety which hangs over us and eats away at us. We can't really put our finger on what it is that is unsettling us inside.

The most important philosopher who has dealt with this anxiety is the German philosopher Martin Heidegger. In 1927 Heidegger wrote one of the most important books of our century, titled *Sein und Zeit (Being and Time)*. We traditionally use the word for *being* to describe the life of a person; he's a human being. The German word for "being" is *sein*. Heidegger does not talk about *sein*. Instead, he talks about *dasein*. In German the prefix *da* means "presence." It can be used to mean "here to there." Heidegger doesn't speak simply about human beings; he talks about human beings *here* or human beings *there*—here a being, there a being, everywhere a being. The idea that he stresses is that the life of every human being is defined by its finite boundaries, *where he is*. He lives his life not in the theater of eternity; he lives it in Philadelphia, Paris, Berlin, or wherever he is. We use statements like, "Here's where it's at." Our life is defined by where we are. In the big picture, Heidegger uses another German word that is very graphic. He said that the reason man experiences anxiety and dread is that man lives in his finite boundaries as a result of what Heidegger calls the experience of "throwness."

Modern man experiences being thrown into existence. We can go to our family Bibles and discover that we were born on a particular day at a particular time in a particular place. We try to convince ourselves that we came into being by an orderly process. But our experience suggests that the process was not really orderly. We feel like we were hurled into the world, just thrown into it. We had no choice about where we were born or who our parents would be. Our existence may be compared to a baby who is thrown into a turbulent sea and told to "sink or swim."

Man has been hurled into an impersonal universe where nobody is at home. We are expected to carve out our own existence and live between twin poles of nothingness. We come from nothing and are destined for annihilation. We understand this intuitively. It eats away at us; we're afraid to talk about it. It produces *Angst*, a nagging anxiety about who we are and why we're here. We are concerned about it, but we see no solution to it.

A final theme found in existentialism is that of freedom in an absolute sense. As Nietzsche's Superman creates a master morality so the existential person must carve out his own destiny by being morally autonomous. He must learn to be a law unto himself. He need not submit to norms because there are no norms. He must have the courage to "do his own thing." He is not only free to do his own thing; he is *responsible* to do his own thing.

"Authentic man" looks into the pit of despair, into the

black void of nothingness, and sees that life is hopeless and meaningless. Nevertheless, he chooses not to succumb to it or surrender to it by seeking the safety of the group and its conventional values and institutions. Instead, he has the courage to exercise his own absolute freedom. He takes sole responsibility for his actions.

The courage for such decisions is a strange sort of courage. The existentialist calls it "dialectical courage." A dialectic involves a severe tension, a tension provoked by an irreconcilable contradiction. Dialectical courage, then, means "contradictory courage." It is contradictory because it follows a bizarre sort of syllogism:

> Life is meaningless.
> We must face life with courage.
> Our courage is meaningless.

We are called to heroic acts of courage with the full knowledge that such acts of courage are themselves meaningless.

"Be of Good Cheer—The World Has Overcome Us!"

Here we see the vivid contrast between pessimistic existentialism and Christianity. Christianity also features a ringing call to courage. The most frequent negative prohibition found in the New Testament comes from the lips of Jesus— "Fear not!" This command is given so often by Christ that it almost seems like a greeting. One gets the impression that virtually every time Jesus appears to His disciples, He begins the conversation by saying, "Fear not."

Here is the difference between the message of Jesus and that of existentialism. Jesus said, "Be of good cheer, for I have overcome the world." The existentialist declares, "Be of good cheer, the world has overcome us."

Jesus gives a *reason* for good cheer. He was not a first-century Good Humor Man spreading sweetness and light with saccharin frivolity, singing, "Pack up your troubles in an old kit bag and smile, smile, smile." His exhortation to joy was based on a real triumph, an ultimate victory He achieved over the threatening forces of chaos.

By contrast the existential cry to courage is based on nothing. It recognizes an ultimate triumph of chaos and clings to an irrational courage. Albert Camus understood this tension when he said that the only serious question left for philosophers to discuss was the question of suicide.

The contradictory character of existentialism was mirrored in the protest movement of the youth counterculture in the sixties. Two slogans became popular: "Do your own thing!" and "Tell it like it is!" On the one hand there was a massive revolt against traditional values and a call to radical subjectivism. The subject does his own thing. There are no objective norms to obey.

On the other hand the summons to the older generation was to objective truth telling. "Tell it like it is!" The slogan suggests that there is such a thing as objective reality, what Francis Schaeffer called "true truth." The youth were angry with their elders for being hypocrites, for living contradictory lives. At the same time the young people were exalting the "virtue" of living contradictory lives.

The contradiction appeared at another level. At the same time the students were denying classical *personal* ethics by embracing the sexual revolution and the drug culture, they were screaming for a lofty *social* ethic with respect to civil rights, world peace, and ecological balance. They wanted a world with love including "free love" with no private responsibility; a world without killing, except for unborn babies, and a world where the environment was pure of toxic substances, except for the ones they used on themselves.

With the impact of existentialism on American culture a serious attempt was made to achieve a synthesis between Christianity and existentialism. Instead of looking to the pessimistic heroes of the movement, the nineteenth-century philosopher Soren Kierkegaard became the focal point of interest. Kierkegaard was seen as the father of Christian existentialism. Kierkegaard's emphasis on personal passion struck a chord in the hearts of Christians. He differentiated among levels or stages of life. The level where most people live is either at a moralistic one or what he called an "aesthetic" level. The aesthetic level is the stage of the observer or the "spectator." The spectator looks at life but stays on the sidelines. He avoids passionate involvement in life.

Kierkegaard understood profoundly that Christianity is not a spectator sport. It demands passionate commitment. Christianity can never be reduced to cold, abstract creeds, or rational systems of doctrine. Truth is not always found in neat packages. It is often paradoxical, according to Kierkegaard.

He spawned on the one hand a renewal of personal commitment to Christ, of Christians plunging into the work of Christ with passion. He also spawned a movement in theology that exalted the irrational. The contradiction became not only acceptable to theologians, but desirable. "Systematic" theology suddenly became suspect because it sought a kind of consistency and coherency that left no room for contradictions.

This new orthodoxy was fashioned along dialectical lines. I once listened to a debate between an orthodox theologian and a dialectical theologian. The latter was blatantly speaking in contradictions to the former's utter consternation. Finally in a spirit of frustration the orthodox man said, "Please, sir, tell me theology once *without the dialectic* so I can understand what you are saying."

The orthodox man was aware that contradictions are unintelligible. No one can understand them, not even dialectical theologians. When we use them we are revealing our *confusion*, not our brilliance.

A final element that grew out of religious existentialism was a new stress on human personal relationships. Martin Buber, a Jewish philosopher, stressed the importance of what he called, "I-Thou" relationships. People are not things. They are not impersonal objects to be studied dispassionately. They are not numbers. We *use* things. People are not to be used. When I relate to another person I am not relating to an "it." Human relationships are to be *subject-subject*, not *subject-object*.

The I-Thou concept helped awaken a new consciousness to people as people. Jews are not cattle to be exterminated by a "final solution." Blacks are not "niggers" to be treated as chattel. Women are not playthings to be used as toys. There must be no such thing as a "Playmate of the Month."

Here was a solid protest against the widespread depersonalization of culture. The theologians who sought to combine existentialism and Christianity gave us a mixed blessing. They were correct in seeing that Christian faith demands personal passion. They were correct in stressing the personal element of human relationships. They were correct in seeing that the Christian faith is more than rationality. Sadly, however, too often they threw out the baby with the bath water. Their protest against rationality became too severe. Their antisystem perspective began to wallow in contradiction.

Surely Christianity is *more* that rationality. But it is not *less*.

Questions for Discussion

1. How do you feel emotionally about the word *futile?*

2. Where do you find expressions of futility in our culture?

3. Where do you observe evidences of a "feeling ethic"?

4. Do you find theology and philosophy cold and dry?

5. Is it easier for you to feel or to think?

6. How is Nietzsche's idea of "herd morality" manifested in our culture?

7. Where do you find expressions of nihilism?

8. Compare the mood of the eighties with that of the forties and fifties.

9. Where and when do you suffer anxiety?

10. Are there contradictions in the Christian faith?

Chapter Four

Sentimental Humanism

IN OUR STUDY of contemporary culture in the United States, we now turn our attention to humanism. Humanism is an ancient philosophy that has gone through many stages and changes. It is difficult to define *humanism* because it is such a broad philosophy and contains so many different elements.

A major problem in understanding humanism is that, as a term, it is often confused with another well-known word, *humanitarianism* Some people use *humanism* as though it were a synonym for *humanitarianism*, but they are very different. *Humanitarianism* refers to a concern people have to care for the welfare of human beings. Anyone who cares about people and who does things to help the cause of people could be called a humanitarian.

Humanism seeks to be humanitarian as well, but humanism, as an "ism," is a philosophy that is much more specific than simply having a care or concern for the welfare of mankind. Judaism cares for human beings; so does Christianity. Even communism, as an "ism," at least expresses a concern for the welfare of mankind. People differ radically as to whether or not it succeeds in its humanitarian considerations, but communism at least professes to be humanitarian. Humanism, however, is a philosophical system and not merely a concern for or an attitude toward the well-being of mankind.

Humanism has a long history. We usually trace its beginnings to ancient Greece, to the pre-Socratic philosopher Protagoras. Protagoras developed a concept of humanism, which he set forth under the motto *homo mensura*. This motto of Protagoras has become a rallying cry for later generations of humanists. It means "Man, the measure." The idea is that man is the measure of all things. Man, in himself, is the ultimate norm by which values are to be determined. He is the ultimate being and the ultimate authority; all reality and life center upon man.

In philosophical language we find another word to describe humanism: *anthropocentric*. To understand this word, let's break it down. From *centric* we get *center*. *Anthropos* comes from the Greek and means "man." For example, *anthropology* means the "study of man." Something that is anthropocentric is centered on man or man centered.

Christianity, by contrast, is "theocentric." It is God centered. In the Christian faith, God is the absolute being and the absolute authority. We can see in this difference of terms an inherent tension between Judeo-Christianity and humanism concerning their center of focus and emphasis.

In history, forms of humanism have subsisted where there was a belief in God. However for the most part God's activity was restricted to being the Creator of the natural realm and natural forces. (The religion that appeared in the older varieties of humanism came in through the door of "naturalism" which says there is a God but not a God who is involved supernaturally with this world.) Earlier forms of humanism acknowledged some kind of power or force from which nature comes, but the center of attention and the center of value was man. It is not the character of God or the being of God that is the measure; man is the measure. Humanism involves a conscious alternative to supernatural Christianity. It sees itself as a competitor to the church. In 1961 the Supreme Court of the United States defined humanism as a religion (*Torcaso v. Watkins*).

There have been many kinds of humanists. There have been optimistic humanists and pessimistic humanists, benevolent humanists with respect to the church and religion, and militant humanists who have vigorously opposed any kind of coexistence with Christianity. It is important to notice that the rallying cry of contemporary humanism tends to be more militantly opposed to the church and to Christianity than were earlier varieties.

In the development of humanism, the sixteenth century was significant. That period witnessed a great debate between two intellectual giants that reflected the struggle going on in Western civilization. These two men, Erasmus of Rotterdam and his antagonist, Martin Luther, represented the conflict between humanism and biblical Christianity.

Erasmus was considered the prince of Renaissance humanism. His motto was the phrase *ad fontes*. *Ad fontes* means "to the source" or "to the sources." What had happened in the Renaissance was the rebirth or the rediscovery of learning. There was a renewed interest in the "golden age" of ancient Greek culture, and a rediscovery of Plato, Aristotle, and the great minds of antiquity. Renaissance humanism went back in history and tried to discover the highest expressions of human culture and to give rebirth to civilization. They returned "to the sources" or the foundation of Western culture.

What is often overlooked, however, is that even though Erasmus wrote satirical essays critical of the Roman Catholic Church, he still remained a member of that church and included the importance of religion in his philosophical system. His call "to the sources" was not merely to renew the study of Greek and Roman theories, but was also to go back to Judeo-Christian sources. He was the one who promoted the movement to recover the ancient languages of the Bible. In fact, Erasmus the humanist was the single most important individual in the reconstruction of the Greek New Testament in his century. This work came to be known as the *Textus Receptus*, which was the Greek text upon which the King James Version of the Bible was based.

Earlier humanists tended to view religion as one aspect of the general growth and development of the human race. Religion was viewed as part of man's experience, part of what it means to be human is to be involved in some kind of religious aspiration. Religion has contributed certain values to the human race. The early humanists saw value in religion, but had no commitment to the absolute authority of the Word of God in the life of the people.

Man-Centered Humanism Versus God-Centered Christianity

The struggle between Luther and Erasmus in the sixteenth century was symbolic of the deeper struggle between Christianity and humanism. We can say that the battle was won by Luther and the Reformation. By the seventeenth century, the tide began to turn. As we move into the eighteenth century and the period of the Enlightenment, we see humanism beginning to prevail over the church as a dominant cultural influence in the shaping of men's ideas. This influence shaped what has been termed "the modern mind." This is important to understand because we are living in a culture in which we are bombarded every day by values and concepts that come out of humanistic philosophy. Keep in mind the fundamental point of antithesis that exists between classical humanism and Christianity, between that which is man centered (anthropocentric) and that which is God centered (theocentric).

The nineteenth century manifested a movement of another kind in the form of cooperation between religion and ancient humanism. We see this particularly in a theology that is called "liberalism." The word *liberal* is a perfectly good word. It means one who is free thinking; one who is open and tolerant; one who is scientific and responsible. Indeed, the word includes all of those elements that we regard from a Christian perspective as being virtuous.

I hesitate to use the word because everyone has a different idea about what it means to be "liberal." There are different kinds of liberals and there are different kinds of liberalism, but when we are talking about liberalism in theology, we are talking about a distinctive movement. In this movement we saw an attempt to reconstruct Christianity on a basis of naturalism. Its thrust was to extract from the New Testament anything that was of supernatural flavor: miracles, the Resurrection, the Atonement of Jesus, the Transfiguration, and the Virgin Birth.

For some reason, a strong focus emerged on the Virgin Birth of Jesus. The debate on the Virgin Birth, however, was not a debate over one small point of Christian faith. It was a debate on principle. It was a debate between supernaturalists and naturalists over the incarnation of Christ. This was the issue that became public, but the nineteenth-century debate was far bigger than the question of the mode of Jesus' birth. It had to do with the clash between biblical, supernatural Christianity and those who wanted to reduce Christianity to its social and ethical aspects.

Emil Brunner, the twentieth-century theologian, said that nineteenth-century liberalism was nothing more and nothing less than *unbelief.* Though Brunner was not an ardent defender of Christian orthodoxy, he was critical of liberalism for going too far. Liberalism had surrendered the essence of Christianity.

Here was the crisis: People came to the conclusion that the Bible did not come by divine revelation but simply reflects primitive man's self-understanding of his religious experience and of his values. The Bible was seen as being interspersed with saga and legend and mythology. It expresses the views found in a primitive people in a prescientific culture.

An entire school of theologians came to the place of crisis. Think about this crisis in practical terms. They no longer believed in the Resurrection of Christ. They no longer believed in the Virgin Birth of Christ. Historically, the church was built upon its outspoken commitment to a supernatural God and a supernatural Christ who was born by miracle, who died a death that is of cosmic significance in atonement, and who was raised from the dead. The New Testament itself says that without the Resurrection the Christian faith is futile. Paul understood this as early as the first century. He said, in effect, "Take away the Resurrection and it's the end of the church." Now there was a group of theologians in the nineteenth century who no longer believed in the Resurrection. What were they to do?

When I went through my ordination on the floor of the presbytery some years ago, one of the fellows who was to undergo this ordination examination with me grabbed me by the sleeve and pulled me aside just before we walked in to be questioned.

"I don't know what to do," he said. "Should I go with the Resurrection or not?"

"What do you mean?" I asked.

He said, "Should I tell them I believe in the Resurrection?"

I asked, "Do you?"

"Of course not," he replied.

His was a moral dilemma and he was asking, "Will the church require it?" The question was not asked in the exam. He came through with flying colors. His discomfort, however, reflected the crisis of the age.

What happens to people in a crisis like that? What do men do if they realize that they do not believe the New Testament portrait of Jesus? Some argue that integrity demands that they withdraw from the church. But the problem in the nineteenth century was not limited to a few people. There is a sense in which, in the academic circles of theology in Western civilization, nineteenth-century liberalism began to control many of the educational institutions. The crisis mushroomed to a grand scale. Liberalism still had a "biblical message." The church had a remarkable platform from which to bring about social change—as an institution it had a place as a part of human culture. Tens of thousands of churches existed throughout the world, representing billions and billions of dollars invested. The church still had an agenda. Clergy still had a function to perform that would keep them gainfully employed. All that was necessary for the church to survive the crisis was a *change of focus*. Now the accent would be on man's condition in this world.

Nineteenth-century liberalism saw a shift of concern from personal, supernatural redemption from sin and alienation from God to what was called "the social gospel." The social gospel extrapolated the ethical teachings of Jesus from the supernatural background of the biblical documents. Those who accepted this social gospel said, "We don't believe in the supernatural, but we still believe in the values and the ethics of the New Testament. The church still has a reason to exist. The church still has a viable ministry to carry on. All we have to do is change the message and change the structure."

Modern Humanism Is Anti-Christian

Not everyone in the church accepted that view, of course. A fierce battle ensued as liberalism in the church brought on the so-called "modernist controversy." It is important to note that humanists and liberals became allies because humanism of the nineteenth-century variety still saw religion as valuable. It saw religion not necessarily as valid but valuable, insofar as it called men toward higher virtues. The humanists embraced important virtues in their commitment to human dignity. They believed in compassion, service to mankind, honesty, industry, hard work, freedom, democracy, and so on. All of these ideals of the humanist were also ideals of the Christian. There was a point of contact and an arena of mutual cooperation.

Modern versions of humanism tend to be more militant regarding Christianity. The clearest statements of the tenets of modern humanism can be found in three brief documents, each about twelve to twenty pages long: *A Humanist Manifesto* (1933), *Humanist Manifesto II* (1973), and *The Secular Humanist Declaration* (1980). All three documents affirm key aspects of humanism:

—the natural world is the only one we can know; the here-and-now is all there is;

—insight, intuition, and divine revelation must be tested by reason; truth is best discovered rationally;

—mankind is the only source of morals and value, and

the highest human achievement is to improve the human condition;

—the future will be better if people proceed ethically and rationally;

—democracy in all aspects of life is to be strived for, as a means of enhancing personal freedom.

If we read these documents, particularly the second and third, we will see in them a spirit of hostility directed against the Christian faith. Why this change from the earlier cooperative spirit?

Since the nineteenth century, various thinkers like John Dewey emerged and said that "religion tends to hinder the evolutionary progress of man." The humanist dream is to rid the world of pain and suffering by man's efforts through education, technology, and industry, but principally through higher education. Religion, in the modern humanist view, tends to keep people in a conservative frame of mind, holding on to outmoded and antiquated values. It tends to make people conservative rather than progressive. At the heart of humanism is a strong commitment to progress.

As humanism has developed it has become organized, with its own meetings and conventions, and its periodicals, such as *The Humanist*. In short, humanism in America is a philosophy, a general attitude, and an organized movement.

Why Humanism Is Irrational

From a Christian perspective, what is the struggle with humanism in our culture? In Western humanism as we know it, the ethics or values of Christianity were borrowed by the humanists and then ripped off their Christian foundation (which is the character of God and the person of Jesus Christ). It is important for us as Christians to be compassionate to the sick and to the poor. We have a duty, a moral obligation, to minister to those people. God has commanded it. But humanism retained these concerns while denying their theological foundations. They want to retain much of the ethic of Christianity while rejecting the Christ of Christianity. They select a portion of Jesus' message while rejecting Him. *The humanist lives on "borrowed capital."* He rejects the foundation upon which his values are established.

Francis Schaeffer said, "The humanist has both feet firmly planted in midair." Schaeffer went on to warn, "Unless humanism is stopped, it intends to beat to death the [Christian] base which made our culture possible."

Basically, the true humanist does not worship. The consistent modern humanist is atheistic. Consistent humanism must be atheistic. Those who still try to worship are often found in groups such as the Unitarian Church. Unitarianism is a clear example of humanistic philosophy blended with religious liturgies. But humanists also worship in the mainline denominational churches. Humanism has had such an impact on our culture that many church members have embraced it without being aware of it.

Humanism is fundamentally irrational. Once its values are stripped from their theological foundation they have no platform upon which to rest except sentiment. The irony of our culture is that humanism has become the dominant philosophy of intellectuals. This is a strange turn of events. It is not by accident, however, that the loudest critics of humanism have been the pessimistic existentialists. Their judgment upon humanism is focused in one word: *naive*. It is a harsh judgment, more than implying that humanism as a philosophy is the quintessence of stupidity. Why?

Examine for a moment (that should be all it takes) the central themes of humanism:

Man is a cosmic accident. He emerges from the slime by chance. He is a grown-up germ. He is moving inexorably toward annihilation. Yet man is the creature of supreme dignity. He lives his life between two poles of meaninglessness. He comes from nothing; he goes to nothing. His origin is meaningless, his destiny is meaningless. Yet, somehow, between his origin and his destination he acquires *supreme dignity*. Where does he get it? Out of thin air.

The thinking humanist (if there is such a thing) must be a nervous humanist. He suffers the tension of the small child who has already eaten his cake and wants it too. What reply can the humanist give to the critic who asks, "What difference does it make if black germs or white germs sit in the back of the bus? Why should we care for the poor? Dignity is an illusion. It is at best a sentimental dream. If I am a cosmic accident why should I not just sleep in tomorrow morning?"

Humanism is intellectually untenable, but it is emotionally attractive. Why? Because we are anthropoids; we are men and women and we want to believe that life has some meaning for us. To the thinking person, humanism gives no reason, ultimately, for ascribing value and values. Values become *preferences* rather than *principles*. The modern humanist recognizes that. He says flatly, "That's what we have. We don't have any principles, we have preferences." My fear of humanism is this: When preferences become ultimate, then whose preferences become ultimate? Historically, in every case, values based simply on preferences end in some form of statism.

The Decisive Battle: Public Education

The focal point of my concern as a Christian comes at this level. The principal vehicle for the dissemination of humanist philosophy is the public school system. This is the clear strategy of the humanist. He insists that the only way we can progress is by educating people. If humanistic philosophy is going to shape the values of modern man it must capture the institutions of education. Humanism has done a masterful job of that capture. Christians, after decades, are beginning to wake up and see that our children are being taught one set of values in the home and in the church, while they get another philosophical system through public education. This conflict is becoming clear with the debates that are raging around the country. It has taken a long time for the Christian community to begin to understand what has been happening. This is where the decisive battle lies in the struggle for the modern mind.

The dominant influence on public school education in the United States today is humanistic philosophy. I am not saying that there is anything necessarily unfair in that, and I am not advocating that the government enforce Christian values in public school education. We can hardly expect a secular state to inculcate Christian values through public education. The values of public education are not created by theologians or the church. Public school curricula are made up largely by secular people with a secular perspective.

Of course, many teachers and administrators in the public schools are Christians. They teach and they make up curricula, but their numbers are becoming fewer and fewer. Their influence is less, as well, because the individual teacher has less and less control over the content of what is being taught in the classroom.

If we tour New England we can experience a visual lesson in American history. The old churches in the old towns are situated in the exact middle of the town. They bear silent witness to a former culture wherein the church was at the center of community life. The first school textbooks were prepared by clergy. The reading primers were made up by Christians. Control of the content of education was basically the will of the community, which was also solidly involved in the church. As the country became more secularized, more of education was removed from the local community. Centrist bureaus sought more uniform standards of curricula and accreditation. If you taught in the classroom twenty-five years ago and told students what Jesus Christ meant to you, nobody would have thought anything of it. If you do that today, you lose your job.

Prayer in public schools has been a controversial topic. When prayer in public school classrooms was ruled unconstitutional, I was delighted. I was one of few Christians at that time who was speaking in favor of getting prayer out of public schools. I wanted it out of the public schools so that people could see that a prayer at the beginning of class on a Monday morning for two minutes, and the reading of the Bible, does not make a Christian curriculum. Such prayer and Bible reading confuse young people. They imply that the humanist education they get all day is sanctioned by God. A whole generation of children was raised to think that what they were learning was Christian education.

I said this in the late fifties and early sixties because I saw that one of the most difficult tasks of the theological educator is not to get new information to people but *to unteach them.* Therefore, I was glad that the battle lines were starting to be drawn. I said at that time that prayer in public schools was unconstitutional by the Supreme Court's definition because the whole issue at that time was whether or not in a democracy, any one group—Jewish, Muslim, or Christian—has the right, through the state, to inculcate in the children its system of thought with state support. That was the complaint of people like Madalyn Murray O'Hair: that tax dollars were being used to support Christian programs in the schools that discriminate against non-Christians. On that point she was correct.

We know that there is no such thing as a neutral education. Remember, humanism was decreed by the Court to be a religion, and, right now, that happens to be the religion in power. The issue, on one hand, is being raised by Christians who want to capture the public school system and make it a channel to disseminate Christian principles to the nation. Another group, also Christian, is saying, "No, what we need to do is to acknowledge the fact that we are living in a nation where there is a separation of church and state and not everyone is a professing Christian. If we want to educate our children in a Christian world view, then we are going to have to have Christian schools." The Roman Catholic Church understood this centuries ago.

What we have now are parents who are Christians who are not worried about educating their children in a humanistic environment. Why? It could be that they do not care what their children learn, but I find that hard to believe. I cannot imagine a Christian parent not caring what his or her child is being taught. What I can imagine is a Christian parent not dreaming that there really is any serious difference between the public school and the Christian life and world view. Christians seem to assume that there is a Christian viewpoint in the public schools when, in fact, it has not been there for decades. It is no longer allowed to be there.

We also have Christian parents who were educated in the public schools who do not realize how much of their own thinking is humanistic. They believe that if public schooling was good enough for them, it is good enough for their children. They send their children back into the system and then wonder why the culture and their own children move away from Christianity and into humanism. A distinctly Christian education is expensive, and many Christians are unable or unwilling to pay the price. The state ultimately controls the education of our children. The only level of freedom we have left with respect to education is to elect to have our own private schools and to be willing to pay the price. To make them competitive means a large expense. Unfortunately, excellence in Christian education is not always a priority for Christian parents. Some would rather send their children to public schools for "free" than to have to spend thousands of dollars a year beyond property taxes to educate their children in a Christian school.

We must remember that humanism is a world view. It shares the skepticism and agnosticism with respect to God found in secularism. It has retained enough common virtues and ideals to be easily confused with Christianity, especially by children. Modern humanism gets progressively more hostile toward Christianity, particularly at the level of public education. It is almost impossible to miss that point in the present cultural climate. The battle between the Christian and the humanist is being fought and will continue to be fought in the arena of education.

The first creed of humanism was not that of Protagoras, *homo mensura*. The first creed was uttered much earlier. Ironically it was not uttered by a human, but by a serpent. His creed was *sicut erat dei*—"you shall be as gods."

Questions for Discussion

1. List some goals and virtues Christianity and humanism have in common.

2. What does it mean to be "theocentric"?

3. How has naturalism influenced modern religion?

4. What is theological liberalism?

5. How crucial is the Resurrection of Christ to your understanding of Christianity?

6. Was Dewey right in saying that "religion tends to hinder the evolutionary progress of man"?

7. How does humanism live on "borrowed capital"?

8. On what foundation does humanism establish human dignity?

9. Why does existentialism consider humanism naive?

10. Is it possible to have a neutral educational curriculum?

Chapter Five

Pragmatism: "Made in USA"

NESTLED IN THE MOUNTAINS of western Pennsylvania is the quaint village of Ligonier. It boasts one of the nation's most beautiful golf courses, the Laurel Valley Country Club, where I've had a few occasions to visit the pro shop. One of the local pros there, John Rock, never greets me by name, but asks when I enter the door, "Does it work?"

My reply is always the same: "Yes, John, it works."

"Then," replies John, "use it!"

This litany has become a tradition with us. I would be shocked and disappointed if I ever walked in the shop and John said simply, "Hello, R.C."

"If it works, use it" is the teaching motto of my golf pro. Never mind the intricate theories of the golf swing. Results are what counts with the man. All of the marvelous theories mean little to the golfer if he slices balls all day.

"If it works, use it" captures the spirit of pragmatism. This is a philosophy that has stamped on its covers, MADE IN USA. The term itself tends to be less obscure than terms such as *existentialism* or *secularism*. The word *pragmatic* is more common in our vocabulary.

Pragmatism is a category of the broad philosophical perspective of secularism which we looked at earlier. While most of the philosophical movements that affect our society have been transported from Europe, pragmatism is home grown. It was born and raised in the United States and reflects something of the genius of American culture with its emphasis on practicality and expediency. If pragmatism had a motto, it would be, "Where there's a will, there's a way."

One man who sees pragmatism as the dominant influence in our society is Dr. Harvey Cox. In his book, *The Secular City*, Cox called attention to the tremendous change that has taken place in Western civilization, a change from a society that looked to God for its values to one that has abandoned the eternal as its point of reference. We no longer anticipate "The City of God"; rather, we look for a present-day "secular city."

In his book, Cox attempted to evaluate American culture according to theological, sociological, and anthropological categories. He made some important observations about our society. He discussed the *shape* of America as well as the *style* of America. He pointed to pragmatism as the dominant influence shaping the American style of life.

Cox wrote, "Urban secular man is pragmatic. He devotes himself to tackling specific problems. He is interested in what will work to get something done. He has little interest in what has been termed 'borderline questions of metaphysical considerations.'"

Modern man wastes little time thinking about ultimate or religious questions. The pragmatist is basically either skeptical or agnostic about man's ability to discover ultimate truth. What the pragmatist says is, "I don't have time in my life to figure out all the mysteries about ultimate reality and ultimate purpose that religion and philosophy have been traditionally concerned about. I have to be busy with living. My life involves encountering a myriad of problems and I need to find solutions to those problems." In other words, the spirit of pragmatism today is the spirit of problem solving.

The realist is portrayed as the man who is asking, "What works?" He is not concerned with what is fancy or pleasing to the intellect in terms of theory. He is concerned with that which brings results.

As a formal philosophy, pragmatism originates from a skepticism about metaphysics or theology. What do we mean by *metaphysics*? It is an everyday word for philosophers, but it is not a word that we find in the daily television soap operas. Metaphysics differs from physics; it is the study of that which is *above* and *beyond* physics. Metaphysics looks beyond what can be seen and observed in the sphere of natural science. It asks questions such as what is ultimate reality? Is there a God? These are metaphysical questions.

For centuries men have sought to unravel the mysteries of metaphysics. During the period of the Enlightenment in the seventeenth and eighteenth centuries, philosophers glorified reason and the scientific method. This was followed by a period of skepticism, particularly during the nineteenth century. At the same time, enormous advances were being made in man's ability to cope with his world. These advances came in the shape of the Industrial Revolution, breakthroughs in science and medicine, and the harnessing of new forms of energy. The hostile forces of nature were being tamed.

We Look to Science to Solve Our Problems

Modern man looks to the scientific community to solve his problems. Cancer, heart disease, arms control, and a sound economy are the issues we are concerned with. We don't look to God to solve our problems. We look to science or government to come up with the solutions.

There is a point of confusion between Christianity and pragmatism. In our common language, we use the term *pragmatic* as a synonym for the word *practical*. We want to be "practical." The desire to be "practical" is as intense among students of theology as it is among engineers. We know that in the final analysis God cares profoundly about what we do. He is concerned about our practice.

The Bible often refers to the importance of our practice. "By their fruit you will recognize them" (Matthew 7:20 NIV). Our *practice* reveals most clearly what we think and what we believe. The pragmatist desires to be practical; so does the Christian. In this discussion, however, we must be careful to distinguish between being practical and being pragmatic; to be practical does not require that we embrace pragmatism as a philosophy of life.

The conflict between Christianity and pragmatism arises precisely at the point of practicality. The issue focuses on the question, "What is ultimately practical?" Ultimate practicality is defined as "practicality in the long run." It is the question raised by Jesus, "What is a man profited if he shall gain the whole world, and lose his own soul?" (Matthew 16:26).

To gain the whole world is practical. It "works" to our advantage to show the whole world as an asset on our balance sheet. Think of the money we could make from rental properties alone if we owned the whole world. Everything looks good until we examine our liabilities. If the words "my soul" appear in the loss column there is not much joy in the profits. Sinners in hell have little interest in the Dow Jones Industrial Average. Gaining the whole world is a short-term matter; losing one's soul is a long-term problem. What seems practical at first glance may be extremely impractical in the final analysis.

The question we must ask is this: Is there a final analysis?

Pragmatism has no room for a final analysis. It shares the skepticism of secularism about the realm of the eternal. Knowledge of the supernatural is closed out to us. The pragmatist is concerned about right now. What works now? Never mind the forever part.

Christianity is rooted in the teaching of Jesus, and Jesus stressed a final analysis, a last judgment where every human being will be held accountable by a supernatural God. When Jesus said, "Take no thought for tomorrow . . ." He was addressing the problem of our human anxieties regarding the future. He was not advising us to ignore eternity.

Recently I was lecturing on the conclusion of the first chapter of the Letter to the Romans. Paul explains that God's judgment is being manifested to the world. Why is it? Because God reveals Himself clearly to all men. Paul declares that man does not see fit to take seriously the knowledge of God he has. *He does not approve the idea of spending much time learning about the character of God.* Therefore, God gives man over to a "reprobate mind" to do those things which are not proper. Paul then concludes the chapter with a catalogue of vices that includes murder, strife, covetousness, gossip, hatred of God, disobedience to parents, maliciousness, malignity, and so on. The apostle makes the point that there is a causal relationship between our thinking and our behavior.

When man will not have God in his thoughts, that lack is immediately reflected in what man does. If we think that God is not worthy of our consideration, then that view will have a major influence on our thoughts and on our style of life.

Not everybody is oriented to theory and speculation. But everybody is involved in practice. Philosophers and non-philosophers alike have to live. We are all involved in the practice of living. But whether we have a sophisticated developed philosophy or not, how we behave is the clearest expression of what our theories really are. No one operates without a theory of life, a system of values. We may not be able to articulate ours; we may not be able to write an essay about it; but we do have a value system. In our minds, we have a theory about what is good and what is not, what is valuable and what isn't, and we act accordingly.

The conflict between pragmatism and Christianity arises because pragmatism is a *theory* of truth. Practicality becomes the key *test* for truth.

Is Truth That Which "Works"?

We have our theories and must test them to see whether or not they are valid or false. The pragmatist's theory of truth is, "Truth is that which works; the good is that which works." Inherent in this view is a skepticism toward ever coming to an understanding of eternal norms.

One of the great ironies of American history occurred at Harvard University in the nineteenth century. Students of philosophy who specialized in concerns of a metaphysical nature formed the Metaphysics Club. Three classmates who were members of that club—William James, Charles Pierce, and Oliver Wendell Holmes—became, along with John Dewey, the leading spokesmen in America for the philosophy of pragmatism. The irony is that, historically, pragmatism grew out of this group at Harvard who were committed to the precepts of metaphysics. The Metaphysics Club produced a violent antimetaphysical philosophy.

Out of a growing spirit of skepticism toward understanding eternal norms, these men began to look for an alternative approach. They said, "We can't know ultimate truth; we can't know ultimate values. We can't go to the other side of the wall so we are stuck by living here on this side. So, how do we know what is right? The answer is by experimentation."

To see how this was applied by one of this group, look at William James, one of the most widely read American philosophers. How did James approach religion? He has written a classic called *The Varities of Religious Experience* in which he analyzes our experience with religious belief.

Suppose you were a Christian and you went to Dr. James to describe your faith. You would go to his study and he would say, "All right, tell me about your Christian experience." You would tell him that you grew up in such and such a home, and that you had a crisis experience when you were twenty-one and were converted to Christianity. He would begin to probe to see how your attitudes changed, how your behavior changed, how your inner feelings changed. He would ask, "Has this been a positive experience for you or a negative one?" You would answer, "It has been a positive experience for *me.*" So James would respond, "For you, religion works. It helps you cope. It helps you make it in this world. So for *you*, religion is *good* and religion is *true.*"

Up to this point, James's analysis says nothing about whether or not there is a God. The earlier pragmatists believed that there was a God but that we could not know very much about Him. They thought that the corporate experience of mankind tended to validate the idea that there was a God. In later periods, pragmatists moved from that view toward a more atheistic bent. Their consistent concern, however, was not whether there is such a thing as ultimate truth (because we can't know it, they said) but rather *what works?* This view embraces a kind of relativism toward truth and goodness.

A student once asked me, "R.C., do you believe in God?"

"Yes," I replied.

"Are you glad that you believe that?"

"Yes."

"Does it make a difference in your life?"

"Yes, it makes a difference in my life. It helps me through all kinds of things."

The student said, "Well, I don't feel the need for God. For *you* God is true. For *me*, there is no God. I don't need God."

What is happening here? Truth is being redefined. Truth, classically, corresponds to objectivity, to what is real. However, in pragmatism, truth is now determined by what works for me or for you. The problem arises when it works for me but it doesn't work for you. Which is true? Well, they are both true, says the pragmatist.

My discussion with the student was not about what works. My discussion was about the existence of God. I was concerned to show that if there is no God then all my praying, singing, and believing could not conjure one up. I do not have the power to create God. I can create religion and my religious experience may be quite meaningful to me. It may "work" in the sense that it provides a bromide to help me cope with life. But it can never work to create a God if, in fact, there is no God.

On the other hand, if there is a God then the student's unbelief or disinterest in Him does not have the power to destroy Him. If the student finds no personal meaning in God, God's life is not thereby in jeopardy. The student is still accountable to God and will eventually face God. What turns the student on has no possible relevance to the actual existence or nonexistence of God.

In pragmatism truth is inevitably relativized. It must be if there is no exit to the ultimate realm of the eternal.

One of the things that bothered John Dewey was the constant accusation by his critics that pragmatism was subjective. He did not appreciate the charge but he was never able to escape it. The criticism was valid. If truth is determined by what works for the individual, then the test for truth ultimately becomes the individual himself.

Pragmatism Focuses on the Short-term

For example, suppose a student is having trouble in college. He has a long-range goal to become a doctor and commences his training to that end, but he begins to struggle and grows disappointed with college. He decides to go out and get stoned on drugs. As soon as he uses the drugs, he is rid of the pain of his depression and is no longer upset about his future. He's floating around in space and if you asked, "Do you think this is good?" he would respond, "Yes, it has solved my problem." This illustrates the second chief criticism of pragmatism, namely that it tends to focus on short-term consequences or on what is expedient.

In pragmatism, as in all world views, truth and goodness are closely related. When the pragmatist declares that something is true because it works he is making a thinly veiled statement about goodness. When we say that something "works," what do we mean? We mean that it achieves a good result. When my car won't start I think that's bad. When it starts I am pleased. I say, "That's good." We assign a positive value to what works. We are saying that it is better that the car starts than that it fails to start.

We won't get much debate about the good result of a car's starting. But matters become far more complex. What is a good economy? How do we know if it is working? Is it good when everybody has the same amount of money or when the money is unequally distributed? We can have an economy where everyone is starving, but they are starving equally. They are equally poor. Or we can have an economy where everyone is eating, but some are eating better than others. Which is better? Our answer will depend on how we define the good. Is good defined by the degree of distribution of wealth or is it defined by the standards of living? How does the pragmatist decide?

"The Greatest Good for the Greatest Number"

At this point pragmatism usually opts for a sister ism called *utilitarianism.* Utilitarianism is concerned with utility, with what is useful. Here the accent is not on the individual but on the group. The slogan of utilitarianism is "The greatest good for the greatest number."

Utilitarianism faces two severe problems. The first is the same problem of defining the "good" as we've already examined. To know what is good for the group may be as difficult or more difficult than defining what is good for the individual. By asking the question, "Good for whom?" we have merely postponed or evaded the question, "What is good?"

The second problem with utilitarianism is the problem of justice. Is justice good or not? Does justice matter? Is justice restricted to the greatest number or is it to be sought for all? Consider this scenario. Three men are in a room. One of them is a farmer who has worked hard to plant his crops and bring them to harvest. His earnings from his crop are $10,000.00. The other two men are bums who have not worked and who have no money. They decide that the farmer should give each of them $5,000.00. They argue that it is good on the basis of utilitarianism. The result is that each of the two bums walk out the door with $5,000.00 in their pockets. The farmer walks out with nothing. We have just witnessed the greatest good for the greatest number. The plan "worked" for the two bums. It wasn't so practical for the farmer. It was the greatest harm to the smallest number. Never mind that justice was denied.

The above parable seems bizarre. It shows a blatant and extreme case of miscarriage of justice. It is an exploitation of the minority by the majority. Yet that sort of thing happens in a utilitarian culture. It is acceptable where the tyranny of a majority is allowed to exist. The parable is lived out every day in the halls of the Congress of the United States. *Where?* In policies of government redistribution of wealth that are based on utility rather than equity. The most obvious example, again, is the graduated income tax. The graduated income tax is in place because it works, not because it is just. It is useful, not equitable.

To say that truth is that which works is not enough. We must have standards or norms that rise above either individual or group preferences. Without such norms tyranny is inevitable, either by the imposition of personal preferences of the individual or the coercive imposition of the preferences of the group. Tyranny is no less tyranny if it is democratic rather than autocratic.

We can see this problem in our national politics. Our political leaders are often influenced by pragmatism. I once spoke at length with a United States senator, discussing several current issues. And I kept asking specifically, "Why don't you do this?"

"Yes, we should do that," he agreed.

"Well, why don't you do that?"

"We can't do it this year," he said.

"Why not?"

"Because it's an election year."

We can't do this, we can't do that. He said it over fifteen times. Finally, out of frustration, I asked, "Senator, is there anybody up on the Hill who thinks in terms of principle rather than in terms of expediency?"

And all he could say was, "I know, I know, I know."

Harvey Cox, in his analysis of American culture, used John F. Kennedy as the image of American pragmatism. Cox traced the image of the ideal political problem solver to the era of Franklin Delano Roosevelt. In Roosevelt's day the nation was paralyzed, caught in the grip of a depression and an economy that had collapsed. The growth and progress of America had come to a screeching halt and the people were selling apples on the streets to survive. Industry was shut down and unemployment was widespread. The threat of war was growing in Europe, and America was in desperate need of leadership.

FDR came into the White House and in the first hundred days of his term passed more legislation than had been passed in the entire term of any prior president. FDR's style was to say, "We have problems. We don't have time to sit around and think through all the long-range repercussions. We must act now. Solve the problems now. People are out of work; we'll put them to work." FDR's style was to solve problems and solve them fast. The accent was on short-term solutions.

According to Cox, Kennedy's style was much the same. Kennedy recognized that the nation was bogged down in problems, and he consciously embraced FDR's "problem-solving" approach. This approach is what we call "Yankee ingenuity."

When I went to live in Europe, I experienced genuine culture shock. We don't realize how strong certain attitudes are in a society until we leave that society. When I went to Holland, I had problems. I got off the boat with no place to live and no job. But I was an enterprising American and I said to myself, "I have a problem. I must find a place to live." So I started looking. I did not realize that I was moving into the most densely populated nation in the world. There are more people per square mile in Holland than in any other nation. As a result, Holland had a severe housing shortage.

As I tried to find rentals, I went to different government offices and heard the same Dutch expression over and over again—*"Niets aan te doen, mijnheer"* ("Nothing can be done about it"), accompanied by a shrug of the shoulders. There was nothing they could do about it. It was the shoulder shrug that nearly drove me crazy. I asked, "What do you mean there's nothing you can do about it? You have a problem? Solve the problem. Don't tell me there's nothing you can do about it. I'm an American; if we have a problem, we find a solution."

In World War II, Hitler never anticipated that any nation could produce 35,000 airplanes in one year. But America did it. That was the miracle of FDR. American production was based on the spirit of pragmatism. The American work ethic is part of it. It has some wonderful virtues associated with it; it is in our blood. If you don't recognize it, visit another culture and you will quickly note its absence. Go to Latin America where everything happens *mañana* ("tomorrow").

As Americans, our motto is "The difficult we do immediately, the impossible takes a little longer." This is part of our national heritage and it is a product of our results orientation. But the problem with pragmatism is the same as that of humanism in that both live on borrowed capital. Even the pragmatists themselves recognize it.

William James said, "Truth is the cash value of an idea." Along the way we select values, not knowing whether they are true or not. We borrow them, and then we try to "cash them in." When they work they have cash value. The difficulty in this whirlwind approach to problem solving is that our quick solutions tend to leave us with new problems.

Social Security: a Pragmatic Solution

During the Depression the nation faced a problem with people who were reaching retirement age without adequate funds to sustain them. To deal with this problem the government initiated an enforced retirement savings plan called Social Security. People began to breathe more easily about their future. They were confident that Social Security would cover their needs. But they failed to consider inflation. When they retired they discovered that the value of the dollar had eroded and they didn't have the security they thought they had. The government made adjustments, desperately trying to catch up until Social Security became the financial elephant that threatened to sink the ship. This predicament did not occur in six weeks; it required decades to mushroom into a gigantic problem. The long-range consequences of earlier decisions began to make themselves felt.

In the field of economics, the expediency of pragmatism has become terribly evident. The result is a government-managed economy. Government-managed economics seeks to supersede or control the natural laws of the marketplace. Government manipulation hopes to avoid the squeeze of abstract principles like the law of supply and demand. If there is a low supply, it can be increased by government intervention. If there is more demand than supply, the government can do various things to increase the supply. If there isn't enough money in circulation, the government can step in and print more.

If we raise ethical questions about such actions, the pragmatist responds in terms of expediency. Again we face the question. Expedient for whom? In the case of manipulating the money supply through government printing of currency, who benefits? The first and most obvious benefactor is the government itself. Why? The government is in debt

—it is in big debt—nay, enormous debt. Here the government can do something "practical" that the private citizen may not do. It can print money. By printing money (with no hard currency behind it) the money supply is increased. When the money supply is increased the net value of the currency is gradually, but inevitably, devalued. This is what inflation is all about.

Consider this scenario: One hundred people live in a closed community where $100.00 is in circulation. The value of each $1.00 is fixed at 1/100 of the supply. The price of goods will be set accordingly. Suppose the butcher incurs a debt of $10.00 to the baker. But the butcher can't pay; he has no money. He decides to remedy his situation by going to his basement where he keeps a covert printing press that spews out intricately counterfeited dollar bills. He prints $10.00. He uses the $10.00 to pay the baker. *Voila!* He is out of debt; he has solved his problem.

"Bad Money Drives Out Good Money"

But a new problem arises. Now there is $110.00 in circulation. What happens to the individual value of the dollar? It decreases by 10 percent. As soon as the community is aware of this, prices rise to adjust. The *inflation* of prices corresponds to the *deflation* of the dollar which corresponds to the *inflation* of the money supply. This is Gresham's Law at work. No government can break Gresham's Law with impunity. Gresham's Law states, "Bad money drives out good money." Look in your pocket or purse for a quarter or a half dollar. Take it out and drop it on the table. What does it sound like? *Clunk.* It doesn't have a nice ring to it, does it? It doesn't sound like silver or gold.

Now empty all your change and find a 1950 quarter. How about a 1955 dime? A 1960 half dollar? Can't find one? Why not? Tons of coins were minted in 1950, 1955, and 1960, and you can find them. Go to a coin-collector store, where they are easy to obtain. But you can't buy a 1950 quarter for twenty-five cents or a 1955 dime for two nickels.

The reason is that our currency has been debased. The government thought that was the practical thing to do. When it mints cheap coins the good coins are driven out of circulation. When it prints "fiat" dollars with no hard currency behind it, the value of hard currency skyrockets while paper currency plunges. The bottom line is higher prices. Gresham's Law.

Again, who benefits when the government does this "expedient" thing?

First, the government. It can pay off its debts with money that is worth less than the money it originally borrowed.

Second, the first people who get the money benefit, if they spend it before the community finds out the dollar has been devalued. (In our closed community the butcher profits and the baker profits if the baker hurries out to spend the $10.00 before anyone realizes what has happened; that is before the prices in the marketplace are adjusted upward.)

Third, the debtors profit. Now, all debts are repaid with devalued money (making thirty-year mortgages on houses very expedient).

Who gets hurt? This process has little benefit for people on fixed incomes—for retired people, and especially for poor people. Normally the poor are the last ones to find out that their meager resources are suddenly worth less. This is why Jimmy Carter said, "Inflation is the cruelest tax of all."

When government manipulates the money supply in this way it is crushing to the nation. What do banks do when they realize people are repaying loans with devalued currency? There is only one thing they can do to stay in business—raise their interest rates. But what does that do for business? Investment capital now becomes very expensive as businesses cut back on employees and inventory and the unemployment rate rises. In a word, the entire national economy takes a beating.

But it takes time before the negative consequences of short-term "pragmatic" solutions are felt. During that time the public becomes confused about the intricacies of what is happening.

Consider another scenario. In 1980 the central issue in the presidential campaign was *inflation*. People were feeling the immediate pain of higher prices and lower purchasing power of their dollars. They wanted a president who would stop inflation.

By 1984 the inflation rate was reduced to 4 percent. The problem was solved. In a poll taken in 1984 only 5 percent of the people were worried about inflation. I was one of them. The vast majority were concerned about other problems—high interest rates, high unemployment, and an annual deficit flirting with $200 billion. (Keep in mind that the first time in American history that the deficit reached $50 billion was during the Carter administration.)

The question the nation then faced was what to do about the deficit? The government had only three alternatives:

1. Cut spending.
2. Raise taxes.
3. Inflate the money supply.

Which of these is politically most expedient? People don't like radical spending cuts. The government fears blood in the streets if cuts are too radical. And raising taxes is never a very popular move, especially when the taxes are already at double the rate where historians argue that people are inclined to revolt. The most enticing short-term solution is to inflate the money supply again. I'm still worried about inflation because pragmatists are running the country. The pragmatist has a tendency to look at the next election. Never mind the next generation.

The Holocaust: a Pragmatic Solution?

For the pragmatists, every end is a means. There are no ultimate goals. Every end is a short-term end, and that end becomes a means to another end, and so on, but you never get to a final solution. It is frightening that the Nazi Holocaust was called by Eichmann "the final solution." The Jewish "problem" was solved by extermination. That was a pragmatic decision.

Too often, when we think only in the short term what is the result? Soon we have not one problem but four. We solve the four and end up with eight. We solve the eight and now we have sixteen. Eventually, by exponential growth, the problems of the culture escalate and explode and bring the society crashing down.

The Bible says truth is that which works, but that which works must be measured by the eternal norms of God. The real conflict between Christianity and pragmatism is the conflict between what is right and what is expedient.

Josiah Roy said, "If you want to see how pragmatism degenerates at the ethical level, consider the oath that a person is required to give on the witness stand in a court of law, and change it to pragmatist categories. 'Do you swear to tell the expedient, the whole expedient, and nothing but the expedient, so help you expediency?' "

It was the philosophy of pragmatism with which Satan tempted Jesus. "Jesus, you are surely not going to go to Jerusalem and go to the cross," suggested Satan. "That's not very practical. It is certainly not the expedient way. Surely there is an easier way to redeem the world."

How else did pragmatism influence the cross? The principal spokesman for pragmatism in the first century was a man by the name of Caiaphas, the supreme rabbi of Jerusalem. What was his advice? Did he not say, "It is *expedient* for us that one man die for the good of the nation"? The Romans must be appeased. He did not ask if Jesus was guilty or innocent or whether this action was right or wrong. He was operating on a purely pragmatic basis.

It is easy to point fingers at Caiaphas and Satan and Karl Adolph Eichmann. If we want to see something disturbing, during one week we should write down every time we make an ethical decision on the basis of expediency. The pressure to do so is overwhelming. We start compromising and then compromise some more until we are merely an echo of everything that is around us. We become part of the problem of human society instead of part of the solution.

Questions for Discussion

1. How do you respond to the word *pragmatic*?

2. How does metaphysics affect your values?

3. Do you think Christianity is practical?

4. Is God concerned about problem solving?

5. What decisions are you making now that will affect you ten years from now?

6. What decisions are you making now that will affect other people ten years from now?

7. Do you have a twenty-year plan?

8. Can God exist and not exist at the same time?

9. How much influence does pragmatism have in education?

10. Where do you see pragmatism operating in politics?

Chapter Six

Positivism: "Seeing Is Believing"

WHEN WE ENTER a discussion on the world view of positivism we are engaging in a topic that few people outside of the academic world are aware of. I am sure that if we took a poll at midday on a busy street corner and asked the question, "What is positivism?" the majority of people would respond that it means "having a positive mental attitude."

Positivism, as a philosophy, has little to do with "positive thinking." Its achitects are not Norman Vincent Peale or Robert Schuller. Its content is not an upbeat antidote to negativism.

Auguste Comte is the person usually associated with the founding of positivism as a philosophy. Comte, a French philosopher, lived during the first half of the nineteenth century. He sought to discover "laws" that he believed governed the development of a society. Although not as well known as Freud or Marx or Kierkegaard, Comte had a vision for the complete reformation of human society. He saw himself as a reformer. He sought to bring about changes that would reflect the progress which Western civilization had undergone. The progress had accelerated through the period of Enlightenment and into the scientific and industrial revolutions of the nineteenth century. Comte wanted to see all of society transformed by a new kind of philosophy that he called the "dominance of scientific knowledge." He wanted to see a culture and a society established *scientifically* rather than philosophically or theologically.

We recall from our previous discussion about secularism the difference between the eternal realm and the temporal realm. The key emphasis of secularism is that man must live his life in the now. Man has no access, no point of entry, to the eternal, transcendent realm.

We mentioned the problem that thinkers have wrestled with throughout history: How do we make sense out of all the particulars that we encounter in our lives? We see dogs, we see trees, we see kangaroos, we see rivers, we see rocks, we see hills, and we see people. Each of these particular entities that appears before us in this world of space and time we call a phenomenon. A phenomenon is a data bit, a unit of experience, that we observe. The word *phenomenon* (or the plural, *phenomena*) has to do with things that we can see, that appear to our senses.

The questions of ancient philosophy were, How does this all fit together? Is there anything that unifies the phenomena of the world that we experience? Historically, men have sought to harmonize or unify all of these data bits by pointing to some kind of transcendent point of unification. For the Christian that one being who makes sense and integrates and coalesces all of the different phenomena is God. The logical answer to sense and coherence is established by the doctrine and existence of God.

Philosophy tries to establish some point of reference in an abstract principle, such as reason or mind. The quest for ultimate truth in philosophy is called the science of metaphysics. It goes beyond the physical realm that we can see and measure. Thus, metaphysics is a philosophical attempt to bring sense and coherence out of all the incongruous elements of this world.

Comte was seeking to bring together the disparate pieces of the social world. He claimed that just as there is a natural law that governs planetary motion, there is also a natural law of society. Just as in biological evolution where there is a movement from the simple to the complex, a movement from the simple to the mature, so also there are similar laws that work in the development of a society.

Comte said that man is going through stages in his own societal progress. He goes through infancy, then through adolescence and then he reaches his adult phase of maturity. This is not only true of individuals, said Comte, but it is also true of societies. His panoramic view of Western history is that mankind has gone through three stages of development. The first stage is the infantile stage where people sought a theological or religious answer to the meaning of life. In the early development of Western civilization, religion dominated the shaping of culture because man superstitiously attributed the unifying force of his world to the person of God. As man began to grow up, he passed through his earlier stage of infancy moving into adolescence. He became a little more sophisticated. He moved away from religion and theology into the metaphysical stage. Now he had a more complex and more abstract system of reason. He can only reach adulthood, however, when he recognizes that the world is to be understood not by religion or by philosophy, but by science. We need a new society established on the basis of science rather than religion or philosophy.

God Cannot Be Known

Comte shared the skepticism of other earlier thinkers. Together they agreed that the whole realm of the eternal or transcendent is unknowable. We cannot get over the wall or around it so that man is left to understand himself and his world on this side of the barrier in the world of phenomena.

There is no "uni" to the "universe." "Universe" is a combination of unity and diversity. The classical model had all of the diversity of this world unified ultimately in God or in some abstract principle. This was not so for Comte. For him there is only diversity, not unity. Science considers simply the particulars of this world. Comte said that there is only one absolute principle and that was that there are no universals. The only absolute, he said, was that everything is relative. So Comte is absolutely saying that there are absolutely no absolutes except the absolute that there are absolutely no absolutes. Everything is relative.

Comte tried to translate this into a workable religion. He tried to establish what he called the "religion of humanity." In the middle of the nineteenth century in London, the positivists who rallied around Comte built what was called the Positivist Temple in Chapel Gate.

Thomas Huxley, the famous English scientist and lecturer, responded to Comte's philosophy by saying, "What he has given Western civilization is simply Catholicism minus Christianity." That was a summary dismissal of Comte's new religion by Huxley. By calling it Catholicism minus Christianity, he was saying positivism was religion without God. It was a religion based upon science and the scientific control of our environment with man at the center.

Logical Positivism

Comte tends to be obscure to the general population, although he must be studied if one is a technical scholar in the history of philosophy. But his impact went far beyond his own personal version of what positivism should look like. One of the dominant forces in philosophy early in the twentieth century was built upon the nineteenth-century foundation of positivism. It was more sophisticated and was called "logical positivism." It became one of the most important and most dominant philosophical movements in this century.

Let me digress here to say that, in my opinion, the two most influential twentieth-century schools of philosophy in our society have been *existentialism* and *analytical philosophy.* If your son or daughter wanted to study in a graduate school of philosophy today, most likely the motif in that school would be what is called analytical philosophy. Analytical philosophy is not the same thing as logical positivism, but it is the outgrowth of it.

Logical positivism emerged as a philosophical force largely in the 1930s and 1940s. It had its roots in a group of thinkers who banded together in Vienna, Austria, in the 1920s, calling themselves the Vienna Circle. The Vienna Circle was a group of European mathematicians, scientists, and philosophers who sought to eliminate the influence of metaphysics and theology on culture. They wanted to free science altogether from any dependence on philosophical systems and allow science to reign supreme. They were convinced, from a scientific perspective, that debating the issue of the existence of God was a waste of time.

There was a sense in which the logical positivists of Vienna tried to cut the Gordian knot and simply say, "All conversation about God, whether He exists or doesn't exist, is meaningless." They believed the very word *God* was a meaningless word.

What Constitutes Meaning?

If somebody came to you and said, "The word *God* is absolutely meaningless," what would you say? Does the word *God* mean anything to you? Many people have died for the sake of the name of God. When you say that *God* is meaningful and the positivist says that it is meaningless, the difference might be because you are working with different criteria as to what constitutes meaning. This is what the logical positivists were trying to do. They were trying to establish the rules of meaning—how we decide whether something is meaningful or not—and they wanted to develop scientific methods to do this.

I once was invited to speak at a church dinner in Pittsburgh. Seated across from me was a warm and friendly professor of physics from Carnegie-Mellon University and during the course of the meal he spoke to me in genuine terms of concern. "It must be difficult for you to be a theologian."

"Why is that?" I asked.

"Because at the heart of everything you teach is God and we can't say anything meaningful about Him."

My response was not what he expected. I did not engage in a defense of meaningful statements of God. Instead I simply replied, "Surely you can sympathize with me since you have an even more difficult problem."

"Oh?" he said. "And what is that?"

"You know. So much of your physics is based on a concept of energy, but you have no idea what energy is."

The professor became amazed. "Nonsense!" he said. "We know perfectly well what energy is."

"What is it?" I asked.

"Energy is the ability to do work,' he replied.

"I didn't ask you what it can *do*," I said. "I asked you what it *is*. You physicists speak of energy as if it were *something*, not just the activity of something else."

"All right then. Energy is mc²."

"Again. I'm not asking for the mathematical equivalent. I want to know what it *is*. What is its being? Its essence?"

"Well," he said, "those are philosophical questions. I can't comment on them."

The great emphasis on logical positivism was the establishment of what was called the Law of Verification. This law, simply stated, is "No statement is meaningful unless it can be verified empirically." (Logical positivism is sometimes called logical or scientific empiricism.)

To verify something means to show that it is true. If someone claims something to be true and that claim can be examined and determined to be true, we say the statement can be verified (shown to be true) or falsified (shown to be false).

How do we verify the truth of the statement, "A triangle has three angles," or the truth of the statement, "A husband is a married man"? We know a husband is a married man because the word *husband* means "a man who is married." A husband, by definition, is a married man. A triangle, by definition, has three angles. I do not have to see one or put one into a laboratory. I don't have to use binoculars or my microscope to find out that two and two are four, because the idea of "fourness" is found in the idea of "two-and-two-ness." Those statements are what we call analytical; they are true by definition.

With analytical statements the subject and the predicate can be reversed without changing the meaning of the statement. Let us examine one of our examples again:

A husband is a married man.

(subject)   (predicate)

In this statement, "husband" is the subject and "a married man" is the predicate. If we reverse the subject and predicate we get:

A married man is a husband.

(subject)   (predicate)

There is nothing contained in the term *husband* that is not already found in the concept *a married man*.

Analytical statements are what we call tautologies. A tautology provides no new knowledge.

By saying that a husband is married, we have not learned anything new. To say that a triangle has three sides means we have not added anything to our knowledge. To add to knowledge, we must synthesize. We have to find out not only that a triangle has three angles but that it is either gold or silver, that it is big or small, or whatever. The idea of bigness or smallness is not found in the word *triangle*. A triangle can be big or small. I can say to you, "There's a BIG triangle out there in the field." If we want to verify that, we will have to look to see whether or not there is a big triangle there.

Let us examine synthetic statements further:

The husband is fat.

(subject)   (predicate)

This is a synthetic statement. The predicate *adds* something that is not necessarily found in the concept of the subject. We cannot reverse the statement and say the same thing.

Fatness is a husband.

(subject) (predicate)

My wife may want to argue this point. She may believe that fatness is the essence of husbandness, but that is because of her limited experience with husbands.

Science is interested in extending our knowledge beyond

analytical statements. It is seeking truth. How do we know if statements are true? It is easy with analytical statements because they are true by definition. Saying "a husband is a married man" is true in the sense that husbands are, by definition, married men. We are still left with a problem: How do we know that there really are such things as husbands? The simple definition of the word *husband* does not guarantee there are, in fact, husbands.

For example: We may define a unicorn as a one-horned horse. We know that all unicorns are horses with one horn and that all one-horned horses are unicorns. But that doesn't mean that unicorns exist. The statement may be logically "true," but we still haven't moved into the world of reality.

Let's take the problem one step further. Suppose we say that:

God is a self-existing eternal being.

What kind of statement is that? It is analytical. It is a tautology. We can reverse the subject and predicate without changing the meaning of the statement. We could say:

A self-existing eternal being is God.

The meaning is the same. But wait a minute. What if there are more than one self-existing eternal beings? That would mean simply that there are two or more gods. If a being is self-existing and eternal then it is entitled to the title *God*. But don't some people say that God is not self-existing and eternal? Don't people worship things that are created? Yes, of course. Lots of things are called God and are not God, but whatever is self-existing and eternal is God (if we define God as a self-existing eternal being).

Does God Exist?

The big question remains. Is there, in reality, such a thing as a self-existing eternal being? What we're asking is, "Does

God exist?" (A major philosophical issue now enters the discussion.) The question is: "Is existence a predicate?"

The logical positivist insists that it isn't. There is a big difference between the mere idea of a unicorn and a real unicorn. The difference between an imaginary unicorn and a real unicorn is the difference of existence.

Is God merely an imaginary idea or a real being? Logical positivism says that we cannot know that merely by thinking about it or talking about it. When we say God exists, we are no longer in the realm of the analytical. Existence adds something new to the idea of God.

Here is the crux of the matter. To say that something exists is to make a synthetic statement. Synthetic statements are not "true" by definition. They must be verified another way. The Law of Verification insisted that statements must be verified empirically or they are meaningless.

What is *empirical* verification? Empirical verification means verification by the senses. That is, to verify something empirically we must be able to see it, hear it, taste it, touch it, smell it. For example, if I say, "There is gold in Alaska," how can we know if the statement is true or meaningful? The statement is not a tautology. The word *Alaska* does not contain within it, necessarily, the idea of gold. Our statement, "There is gold in Alaska," means that real gold *exists* in Alaska. To verify the statement we must find gold in Alaska that we can see or touch.

To falsify a statement can be easy analytically but very difficult synthetically. For example, if I say a triangle has four sides or a husband has never been married (not even by common law) my statements are falsified. They are false by definition. It is like saying, "The circle is square."

When we move to the realm of the synthetic, matters become more difficult. Suppose I say, "There is gold in Antarctica." Now I have big trouble. I can verify the statement if I find gold in Antarctica. If I find gold the statement is proven true. But what if I don't find gold? How much of Antarctica must I examine before I can say, "There is no gold in Antarctica"? Every square inch. But suppose I do that and find no gold. Has the claim "there is gold in Antarctica" been falsified? No. It has not been verified, but it has not been falsified either. Perhaps in my examination of Antarctica I overlooked something. We can never falsify the possible existence of something empirically because our empirical powers are always finite and subject to error.

But simply because something has not been falsified does not mean that it is thereby verified. Christians need to learn this. Often we hear the debate about the existence of God go something like this: The skeptic says to the Christian, "You cannot prove that God exists." The Christian responds, "You cannot prove that He doesn't exist." Such a response is a cop-out by the Christian. The Christian should take little comfort from the idea that the nonexistence of God cannot be proven.

We cannot prove that ghosts who are allergic to scientists and all scientific instruments of detection do not exist. But no one can verify their existence either. We can structure our definition of ghosts or of God in such a way that it is neither possible to verify or falsify their existence.

What logical positivism tried to do to was establish the rules of verifying truth and meaning. The Law of Verification was their golden rule. Statements were regarded as being meaningful *only* if they were analytically true or could be verified empirically. The statement "God exists" was judged meaningless because it was incapable (in their judgment) of being verified logically.

The problem with the Law of Verification was that it was too narrow. It was too restrictive. Statements like "I love you" cannot be verified empirically, but people consider them meaningful. However, "I love you" is not the sort of statement the scientists were concerned about. It is an emotive statement.

A Positivist House of Cards

The most severe and ultimately fatal problem with the Law of Verification was that it said too much. It ruled out too many statements as meaningless. It was literally suicidal. It killed itself. If the only statements that are meaningful are those that are analytical or can be verified empirically then what happens to the Law of Verification? The Law of Verification itself is neither analytical nor can it be verified empirically. Therefore it must be judged meaningless. It is ironic that the cardinal rule of meaning according to positivism was itself unverifiable and meaningless. The positivist house of cards collapsed by its own weight.

Though philosophers have largely rejected the narrow Law of Verification it has made an enormous impact on our culture. We have seen a generation of theologians go through the terrible crisis of having to determine whether or not any statements about God are meaningful or are simply emotive (that is, saying something about you and your emotional makeup), rather than scientific.

A crisis of faith and science has emerged that has shaken our culture. At the popular level of culture we live with the slogan "seeing is believing." A kind of religious aura has surrounded the scientific community. Physicians have become the new high priests of the culture. Psychiatrists have become the new experts on morality. Ethics itself is being reduced to measurable feelings. Guilt itself is becoming a crime.

A battleground has emerged between the Christian community and a kind of scientism. We see it in the fierce debates over evolution versus creationism in the public schools and in court decisions regarding abortion. Who decides when life begins? Life has lost its theological definition. Unborn babies are considered meaningless blobs of protoplasm.

For the most part the Christian community has surrendered science to the pagan. Logic, reason, and empirical investigation are the tools of the "world." The Christian lives sheltered in his fortress of faith. A recent novel contained dialogue between a scientist and a priest. The narrator commented, "The scientist set forth his reasons and the priest confessed his faith."

In this scenario reason and faith are enemies. The Christian is called to choose faith over reason. We call this "fideism" or "faithism."

An appeal is made to the New Testament to justify the unconditional surrender of reason and empirical evidence. The Bible says, "Faith is the substance of things hoped for, the evidence of things not seen" (Hebrews 11:1).

In this passage faith is contrasted with evidence in things that are seen. On the basis of this passage some have concluded that:

Faith = belief in things unseen
Knowledge = evidence of empirical things

The conclusion then is that "All faith is based on something other than empirical evidence."

Thomas is viewed by the fideist as the original logical positivist. He invented the modern creed when he declared "Except I shall see in his hands the print of the nails, and put my finger into the print of the nails, and thrust my hand into his side, I will not believe" (John 20:25). Thomas was from Missouri. For him, seeing was believing. He viewed faith as something to be based on evidence, not something to be believed against the evidence. He saw a radical difference between faith and credulity; between faith and fideism.

What was Jesus' response to Thomas? He said, "Because you have seen me, you have believed; blessed are those who have not seen and yet have believed" (John 20:29 NIV). Here the words of Jesus seem to carry at least a mild rebuke.

This encounter certainly seems to suggest that something is wrong with demanding evidence for faith and something virtuous about believing without evidence. But does it really? The entire ministry of Jesus was ablaze with empirical evidence. He did miracles which were "signs" of His identity. Peter declared, "For we have not followed cunningly devised fables, when we made known to you the power and coming of our Lord Jesus Christ, but were eyewitnesses of his majesty" (2 Peter 1:16). John wrote, "We *beheld* his glory" (John 1:14, italics added).

Jesus Appealed to Empirical Evidence

The biblical record of the existence of God and the truth claims of Jesus appeal again and again to empirical evidence. It is based on what is seen with the eye and heard with the ear. Why then does Hebrews speak of faith as evidence of the unseen?

The author of Hebrews had no intention of divorcing faith from reason or faith from empirical evidence. Faith is based upon evidence; it is based upon what is seen, but it goes beyond what is seen. In summary it works like this. We trust Christ, who is seen, about matters which are unseen.

God displays Himself in creation. He reveals Himself in history. History is the arena of the seen. But much remains unseen. For example, I cannot see tomorrow. No crystal ball is strong enough to see the future. But God knows the future. When God tells us about the future we trust that what

He is saying is true. We cannot see it. We have no empirical data available to us from the future. But we believe God's Word about the future because in the past He has proven Himself, both rationally and empirically to be utterly trustworthy. Our faith in the future is established by the evidence of the past. Scientific predictions can and have been wrong. God's predictions cannot be and have never been wrong.

To trust God in matters of things unseen is not a matter of blind faith. It is not credulity. It is a reasonable faith. Indeed, to not believe one as well as attested as God for the future is to crucify the intellect. It is foolish not to trust Him when He has evidenced Himself to be utterly trustworthy.

In the final analysis positivism offers a truncated science, a science so limited in scope that it ignores the wider realm of truth. It seeks to make science independent of other closely related fields of inquiry. It cuts us off from ultimate meaning. If that is what Comte meant by cultural maturity it means we pay an awfully high price to grow up.

Perhaps a second glance at history shows the rejection of faith not as a move from infancy to adulthood, but merely as another example of adolescent rebellion, a teenage temper tantrum.

Questions for Discussion

1. Has modern man reached the point where religion is no longer a necessary part of life?

2. What is "practical atheism" as differentiated from "theoretical atheism"?

3. Why do some people say the word *God* is meaningless?

4. How does science define gravity? Space? Motion? Light?

5. What is the difference between verification and falsification?

6. What is tautology? Give some examples.

7. Why is it impossible to falsify the existence of God?

8. What is fideism?

9. How is faith related to reason?

10. Why did the Law of Verification collapse?

Chapter Seven

Pluralism and Relativism: "It's All Relative"

As MISSIONARIES ATTEMPTING to understand the way of thinking in our culture, we must turn our attention to twin topics under the umbrella heading of secularism—pluralism and relativism. Let us think once more of the high wall we examined earlier, the wall representing the line of demarcation separating the present time from the eternal world. It is the barrier to the transcendent realm of unity, the wall that confines and restricts us to this time and this place.

We are cut off and isolated from any contact with the eternal world. The transcendent realm is where we find unity. The world in which we live is the world of diversity. Universals are beyond the wall; the particulars of our experience are here and now. The transcendent realm is also the realm of the absolute. This side of the wall is the place of the relative.

Unity	Universals	Absolutes
	W A L L	
Diversity	Particulars	Relative

The basic idea of pluralism is this: We have diversity here in this world. We have no access to ultimate unity, no way to bring the diverse things of our experience into a coherent whole. We have particulars but no universals; relatives but no absolutes.

Printed on our currency is the motto of the United States of America, *E Pluribus Unum*—"From the many, one." It calls attention to the dream of our forefathers, that people from diverse ethnic and religious backgrounds could come to this country from all nations of the world and form one nation. Out of that plurality and diversity of background, unity was to emerge. The idea expressed in our Constitution and in the Declaration of Independence was straightforward: We would have one nation under God. The original assumption of our forefathers was the conviction that there is a transcendent being; transcendent truths would be the basis by which all these disparate groups and ideas were to be unified.

In our present concept of pluralism, we have taken a significant step away from the original idea upon which this nation was founded. Originally, the idea meant to take from the diversity or the plurality and to bring them together into harmony. Now, modern man is saying that he is cut off from God, cut off from the transcendent point of unity. All we have left is plurality. The new motto for this understanding of the culture would read something like *E Pluribus Plurus*—"From the many, many."

In discussing plurality and pluralism, we must distinguish between the two. To speak of a plurality is simply to say there are diverse ideas or peoples or backgrounds. However, as soon as we add that suffix *ism* to the word *plural*, we are saying something different. We are now saying that plurality is all that there is. There is plurality but no unity; there is nothing that brings ultimate coherence.

It's fascinating to recognize certain buzz words that come into fashion from time to time. In the nineteenth century, the word *evolution* was used as the "open sesame" to a cave full of problems. When we think of evolution, the sciences of biology and anthropology usually come to mind. Evolution is a scientific term to describe the progressive development of a species from its origins. In the intellectual world of the nineteenth century, however, the concept of evolution was not restricted to biology but it was applied widely to many endeavors. All of history was suddenly interpreted in light of the general scheme of evolution. There was a belief in the movement from the simple to the complex, from the primitive to the sophisticated.

Theology was examined in the nineteenth century through the lens of evolution. In the "higher criticism" school of biblical scholarship, biblical religion was viewed as a gradual development from a primitive belief in many gods to a higher view of monotheism. This perspective saw the belief in one God as a late development in the history of religion. It was thought to be as recent as the eighth century B.C. with the advent of the Old Testament prophets. Moses, it was said, was not really a monotheist and Abraham was a myth.

The evolutionary approach to the Bible speculated that Jewish religion followed the general pattern of development that went as follows:

animism——polytheism——henotheism——monotheism

Animism: In this schema all religion is said to begin with animism. Animism is the notion that apparently inert objects are inhabited by spirits. They are "animated." Trees, rocks, totem poles, and even certain animals are worshiped because they are indwelt by spirits. Normally these spirits are evil spirits. The job of religion is to make peace with the spirits, to ward off their evil power. Primitive people place offerings before these objects, chant to them, and do religious dances around them.

Polytheism: The second stage of religious evolution is polytheism. Here the "gods" have separate identities. They are not mere spirits inside of rocks or crocodiles. They normally have a special abode in the sky or on a distant high place such as Mount Olympus. Each nation has its own set of gods and each god has his or her particular function. Think, for example, of the gods and goddesses of Rome and Greece:

	ROME	GREECE
God of War	Mars	Ares
God of Love	Venus	Aphrodite
God of Wisdom	Minerva	Athena
Queen of Gods	Juno	Hera
God of Purity	Vesta	Hestia
King of Gods	Jupiter	Zeus
God of the Sea	Neptune	Poseidon
Messenger God	Mercury	Hermes

Other cultures had similar pantheons. We find them in Egyptian religion, Persian religion, and throughout the ancient world.

Henotheism: Henotheism is a transition stage in the ladder of evolutionary development. It is a sort of halfway house between polytheism and monotheism. Henotheism has one god for a nation or ethnic group. Though many gods exist, each of the gods has his own sphere of dominion. For example, the evolutionists think they observe this in the Old Testament where Jehovah is seen as the national god of the

Jews. The other nations have their own territorial gods as well. The Caananites had Baal and the Philistines had Dagon. These gods enter into the battles between the nations.

Monotheism: As the word suggests, monotheism reduces religion to one God who is supreme. He is a high god. He rules over all nations. There are no territorial or ethnic limits to His dominion. He rules over all human activities such as love, war, harvest, and the like. This is the latest and final stage of religious evolution. It is alleged to have come much later than the book of Genesis. The idea that Jehovah was the Creator of the whole world was viewed as a later insert addition to the Jewish writings, a rewriting of their own history by which later monotheists wrote their religion backwards into this history.

Not only did evolution influence theology but it also affected theories of politics, economics, and philosophy. All of these disciplines came under the influence of this all-embracing concept during the nineteenth century.

Our Lives Have Been Changed by the Threat of Nuclear War

In the twentieth century, the buzz word that replaced *evolution* was *relativity*. We are all aware of the changes in our lives that have been brought about by the scientific revolution based on Einstein's theory of relativity. This is the atomic age. Our lives have been changed by the threat of nuclear war as well as by new possibilities of power from nuclear energy that exist as a result of Einstein's work.

From the viewpoint of science, relativity simply has to do with description of motion. We can say that motion may be considered from more than one reference point. If I am moving toward you, it does not matter whether my motion is considered from my perspective or from your perspective. We simply have different reference points. In this, there is a sense in which my motion is relative. It is relative to a particular reference point. Thus, relativity in motion is defined or determined by various reference points.

There is a big jump, however, from relativity to relativism. It is one thing to say that motion is relative to a reference point; it is another thing to say that *everything* is relative. We have all heard the statement, "Everything is relative." We may even say it. If we do, we are perpetrating a myth of contemporary culture. I call this a myth because it couldn't possibly be anything else. If everything is relative to everything else, then there is no ultimate reference point. There is no basis for truth. If everything is relative then the statement, "Everything is relative," is also relative. It cannot be trusted as a fixed truth. All statements become relative. All axioms become relative. All laws become relative. Relative to what? To other statements, which are also relative. We have infinite relatives with no ultimate reference point. We have millions of "children" with no "parents." Truth is quicksilver.

Some view ultimate or "absolute relativity" (a contradiction in terms) as a major advance in modern science. In reality it is the end of science; the final graveyard of truth. It is one thing to say that for mathematical purposes motion may be considered as relative. But if everything is relative including ethics and values then we are in deep weeds: the kind of deep weeds one finds in a jungle. Consider relativity in ethics. If I don't like you and decide to murder you, is that good or bad? Neither. Or both. It's relative. For you and your family—your relatives (sic)—it may be considered bad. For me it's good since I've destroyed a personal enemy. In a relativistic law court why should a judge find against me? To call my act of murder "bad" would be an arbitrary judgment if everything is relative.

That is precisely where modern secular man finds himself. He lives his life with no ultimate, fixed, and absolute reference point that can define his life or the meaning of his existence. If everything is relative, you are relative, and there is no substance to the meaning of your life. The crisis in pluralism is that there is no ultimate point of reference.

In relativism, there are particulars but no universals, relatives but no absolutes. This means that we can have values but no Value, truths but no Truth, purposes but no Purpose. That is, we have no fixed standards by which to measure or to judge values, truth, purpose or beauty. Once we embrace relativism we live in a world of ultimate chaos.

Let me try to make this more concrete and relevant to where we live by looking at the effects of relativism in theology, in education, and in social ethics.

Pluralism in the Church

The tragedy of our day is that pluralism has not only been accepted as a working ideology in secular culture, but it has also been widely embraced in the church. You may have heard a congregation or a denomination proudly claim, "We are a pluralistic church." This means that church welcomes all different kinds of theology and viewpoints. It is not merely a matter of diversity within unity.

The Bible describes the church as a body. It is made up of diverse parts. Each part has an important role to play, an important function to perform. Just as the human body needs eyes and ears and a mouth, so the church needs various parts to it. We have different gifts, different tasks, different personalities. Yet in this diversity is unity. We have one Lord, one faith, one baptism. Ideally, we would all believe the same thing, but we do not all have a perfect understanding of the Bible. The Bible calls us to be patient, tolerant, and kind to one another in many points of disagreement. Yet there is an essential unity in truth. Certain truths cannot be negotiated. Denials of *essential* truths of Christianity are not to be tolerated in the truth.

Pluralism suggests more than just diverse opinions in the church. It allows contradictory views of Christ, of God, and of the very essence of the Christian faith. It considers them all to be right. Once a church embraces pluralism it is saying, "It doesn't matter whether we agree on the essential points of the Christian faith, because it's all relative."

Pluralism: The Antithesis of Christianity

Some time ago I spoke at a meeting of religious leaders and I told them, "If anybody comes to you and tries to sell you on the virtues of pluralism as a basis for church renewal, run for your life. Pluralism, as a philosophical idea, is the very antithesis of Christianity. No church can survive for long in that kind of chaos."

When I finished with my address, one of the members of the group stood up and started to speak in favor of pluralism. To avoid hypocrisy, as soon as he started to talk in favor of pluralism I ran from the podium and out the door. Needless to say, this was to everyone's consternation. I left hundreds of people looking for a speaker who had just vanished. Finally, I popped my head back in the door and said, "I just told everyone ten minutes ago to run for your life if anybody tries to persuade you about the virtues of pluralism, so I had to demonstrate it myself." I hope they got my point.

Let me illustrate the problem of relativism in schools. I can remember when my daughter entered kindergarten for the first time. It was at a progressive school in Boston that had a sophisticated curriculum. At that moment I realized there was a sense in which her mother and I were no longer the primary influence on the shaping of her mind and her ideas. Now she would be sitting under someone else's tutelage for six or seven hours a day in a public school system. That is a traumatic thing for those parents who are concerned about the development of the mind of their child. I wanted to monitor closely the education that she was getting.

She came home after kindergarten and I asked her, "What did you do today in school?" She answered, "We played with a puzzle and we worked with modeling clay." I thought, "That doesn't seem too dangerous."

After about six weeks, we received a notice inviting us to an open house for parents where the principal of the school would explain the curriculum. My wife and I went to that open house. The principal of the school was a congenial and articulate man who desired to put our fears to rest. He said, "I know you parents are feeling the loss of your role in the education of your children. We want you to understand that everything that is done in this school is done with a carefully thought-out purpose." He then unveiled the curriculum in a way that astounded me.

He said, "From 9:00 A.M. until 9:17 A.M. every morning, the children play with these puzzles." He held up the puzzles. He continued, "I know when your child comes home from school, you ask, 'What did you do today, honey?' and your child says, 'We played with puzzles.' You probably think that all they're doing here is having a good time and that we're merely sophisticated baby-sitters.

"I want you to understand that these puzzles were created by a team of expert neurosurgeons. They were designed in such a way as to develop the motor muscles of the last two fingers of the left hand." I thought, "Wow!"

The principal continued with the schedule. "From 9:17 to 9:32, they are involved in this particular activity. This activity was put together by a group of researchers at a midwestern university." He proceeded through the entire curriculum and his evident point was that every single dimension of that curriculum had a specific purpose; nothing was left to chance or arbitrary action.

After he was through, I was overwhelmed. He then smiled and asked, "Are there any questions?" The response of the audience was spontaneous laughter as if to say, "Who's going to ask any questions about this? We can't believe it."

Instead of questions the audience broke out in spontaneous applause. I raised my hand. The principal acknowledged me and I asked, "You have carefully explained that every item in this curriculum has a specific purpose attached to it, and I'm impressed by that. My question is, 'What is the overarching purpose of the curriculum?' You have only so many hours in a day and there are only so many possible individual purposes that you can implement in the curriculum. You have to make a decision about what goes into the curriculum. Therefore, you must have some overarching blueprint that governs the selection of the individual and particular purposes that you have in the curriculum. What I'd like to know is what is the overall purpose? If I put it another way, what kind of child are you trying to produce?"

His face became beet red. He looked at me in obvious discomfort and said, "I don't know. No one has ever asked me that question." His reply was stated in genuine humility. He was cordial. His voice signaled no hostility. I said to him, "I deeply appreciate your honesty. You gave me a candid answer. I thank you for that, but I must confess that your answer terrifies me."

The Boston school curriculum had numerous *purposes*, but no stated purpose. It was quite efficient, but to what end? The question we must raise with relativism is, who decides what is important? On what basis are decisions made? Let me illustrate the importance of this from a current controversy in our society.

Relativism and the Issue of Abortion

One of the most controversial issues of our day is that of abortion. It is tearing this country apart politically, economically, socially, and in every other way. Legislation is pending in every statehouse over the question of abortion. The issue is not whether or not it is all right to have an abortion if a person is subjected to rape or if the mother's life is in danger. Those are moral questions that theologians and students of ethics work with. The issue today is over the question of abortion on demand.

This issue has drawn sharp lines between people. On the one hand are those who vehemently oppose abortion on demand; they have initiated the movement called "pro-life." On the other hand is a group of equally committed people in favor of abortion on demand, called "pro-abortion." In the middle is a mass of people who call themselves "pro-choice."

Legislatively, the difference in our society is determined by this middle group. Consistently we hear people from this group saying, "I personally would not choose to have an abortion, but I believe every woman has the right to make that choice for herself." On practical, legal or legislative levels, there is *no difference* between pro-choice and pro-abortion. *A pro-choice vote is a pro-abortion vote.* A vast number of mainline Christian churches have gone on record adopting this pro-choice position.

The issue goes deeper than that, however. The question

we must face is, does anybody ever have a right to do that which is wrong? When we ask this question we must ask, what kind of right? Legally, we have the right to be wrong. In our country I may disagree with you, but I will defend to the death your right under the law to state your views. The concept of certain rights of freedom, including the freedom to be wrong, is very important to our society as a tolerant democracy. We have a *legal* right to be wrong, but does God ever give us a *moral* right to be wrong?

We must distinguish between legal rights and moral rights. We may claim that the pro-choice position is an argument for legal rights, but, in actuality, we are talking about moral rights. If the issue is whether or not there should be a legal right for a person to choose abortion, we are begging the question by saying, "My argument for having a legal right is that I have a legal right." Behind the philosophy of pro-choice is the idea that everybody has the moral right to choose for themselves to have or not to have an abortion.

Who Gives You the Right to an Abortion?

Now I want to ask this question: Where does that moral right come from? I have yet to hear anyone raise that question, nor have I seen it in the press. Today everybody is talking about rights. There are women's rights, prisoners' rights, children's rights, and so on. The question is, "Where do we get these rights?" What is the foundation for a right? Is it natural law? I would not want to defend the right for abortion on the basis of natural law. Is it a right that is given to us by our Creator? Does God give us the right to choose abortion? Does nature give you the right? Who provides the right? The concept upon which this large group of people build their argument has no foundation. Before we claim a right, we should be able to state where that right comes from.

To continue with this illustration of the abortion issue in our discussion of relativism, I could ask the pro-choice people what it is they are really saying. What is their claim based on? The answer would be preference. They want to be able to choose. It is one thing to say I want something. It is totally different to say I have a right to it. It is strange that this position emerges in a context of pluralism and relativism, because it comes from the idea that no one in a relativistic society ever has the right to impose his standards on somebody else. Why not? Because everything is relative. Abortion is relative to each individual. If you want to have an abortion, you have the right, say the pluralists. You have that right because morality is relative in a pluralistic society. The one thing that our country cannot tolerate is one group of people imposing its views upon another group.

In pluralism, a view of toleration emerges with a subtle shift. In classical thought, toleration, patience, and longsuffering with people who differ from us were Christian virtues. God's law requires that we be tolerant and charitable with each other. But it is one thing to say that all different views are tolerated under the law; it is a short step from there to say that all different views are equally valid. Pluralism says not only are all views equally *tolerable* under the law, but all views are equally *valid*. If that is the case, then we are saying that every view has as much validity as its contradictory, in which case truth is slain. We can have truths, but truth is impossible. Once you realize that you have destroyed truth, even truths are not true, values have no value, purposes have no purpose, and life becomes impossible.

We can argue the relative merits of Confucianism and Christianity, but they can't both be true at the same time because they conflict. We can argue between Buddhism and Judaism. They can both be wrong, but they can't both be right about the ultimate issues in which they differ.

Relativism Ultimately Results in Statism

Pluralism and relativism have no possibility of being true because, from the beginning, the very possibility of truth itself is eliminated. If everything is true, then nothing is true. The word *truth* is now empty of meaning. That is why modern man finds himself in a dilemma. He is thrown into chaos long-term, and man cannot continually live in intellectual chaos. There is a sense in which our present culture, more often than in any other period in history, is "up for grabs." When this emptiness has happened in the past, something has come to fill that vacuum. Relativism is ultimately intolerable. What will come to this vacuum is some form of statism because something has to bring unity. The good of the "state" will become the ultimate point of unity.

The rapid growth of the centralized state is happening before our eyes in the United States. Consider the areas in which the state functions today where it did not function thirty years ago. Consider the areas where the people of America formerly looked to God for their security, their meaning, and their decision making and now, instead, they look to the state. This eventually becomes statism, where the state becomes the *goal* of life. The state becomes the reason for us to live. The state unifies, transcends, becomes absolute, and is eternal.

The state steps in and says we are going to be united. How? By going to the same schools, by learning the same things, by saying the same words. At the extreme, look at the nation of China, a uniformity by enforced unity. We may say that is the very opposite of pluralism. No, that is the *result* of pluralism. That is the result of the loss of transcendent unity. The God whom we worship is a God who brings unity, but at the same time preserves diversity. We all have a sinful tendency to force everybody else to conform to us. Even in the church we see this tendency. I am a teacher and I want to exalt teaching as the only significant gift of the Holy Spirit. You're an evangelist and you have no time for the teacher. Yet God has said one body, one Lord, one faith, one baptism—but a diversity of gifts and talents, a diversity of personality. Your humanness is beautiful in the intricacies of its diversity, but your humanness also finds an ultimate point of reference in the character of God. Take away that ultimate reference point and humanity itself is demeaned.

We cannot live on this side of the wall alone. We are going to either have God on the other side of that wall or we will substitute the state in His place. I challenge you to find one culture in the world where that has not happened. That's what terrifies me.

The American government faces a serious crisis. People are demanding from the state more than the state can give. People are looking to the state for salvation. Unfortunately, the state does not have the equipment to save a fallen race. The state exists on this side of the wall. It can never provide ultimate unity for our plurality unless it becomes *absolute*. Relativism provides a moral vacuum that screams to be filled. As nature abhors a vacuum, totalitarian governments love one. They rush in to fill a vacuum.

Questions for Discussion

1. What is the difference between plurality and pluralism?

2. Why is ultimate unity on the far side of the wall?

3. How has "evolution" served as a buzz word?

4. What is evolution? List three arguments for the evolution of man.

5. How does the church exhibit unity and diversity?

6. What is the purpose of your business? Your school? Your church?

7. What is the practical legal difference between pro-abortion and pro-choice?

8. What is the difference between a legal right and a moral right?

9. How much involvement does the government have in your life?

10. What kind of people like to *control* other people?

Chapter Eight

Hedonism: "Grabbing for All the Gusto!"

SOME AMERICANS have never heard the word *hedonism* but few have not experienced the impact of the philosophy of hedonism on their lives. As a world view, hedonism has as its basic principle the belief that the good and the evil are defined in terms of pleasure and pain. Man's ultimate purpose for living is to be found in enjoying pleasure and avoiding pain. The hedonist's constant goal in life is to pursue those things which increase pleasure and decrease pain.

Hedonism is not new. Historically, its roots go to the earliest times of recorded history. We could trace it to the Garden of Eden if necessary. In formal philosophy, however, hedonism can be traced to the ancient Greek culture, to the school of the Cyrenaics in the late fourth century B.C. The Cyrenaics were what we might call crass hedonists. We have probably seen their philosophy of life portrayed on film, in scenes of Roman orgies in which people indulged themselves in wine, women, and song with reckless abandon. Fellini's film *Satyricon* was perhaps the most vivid portrayal of this kind of life-style that Hollywood has ever produced. In ancient times, pagans had a festival of celebration for the god of wine, Bacchus. Indulgence was the byword as Bacchus was honored by a wild orgiastic celebration.

Hedonism not only became a philosophy in parts of the ancient world, but was actually elevated to the level of a religion. Dionysius was worshiped by means of a frenzied orgy also. He was honored as the one who would give us the ability to break free from the chains that inhibit us. These chains were to be found in our normal states of consciousness and awareness. The Greek philosophers understood that there were limits to what we are able to know through the use of our senses. There was also a limit to the knowledge that we could attain by speculation on the basis of reason. Some sought release from the normal restraints of human knowledge by means of intuition or mystical experience while others worshiped the god that they thought would give them the ability to transcend the normal limits of consciousness. Dionysius was the god who provided the means. In the state of drunkenness a person became free of the normal inhibitions of waking life. People believed that in a drunken stupor they could make contact with the supernatural world during their mystical experience of "euphoria," an experience called not "getting low," but "getting high." This meant breaking through the limits and the structures of normal consciousness. Added to this was an array of sexual involvements including temple prostitution. The prostitutes were able to help a person break down his inhibitions so that he could make contact with the gods and experience the feeling of ecstasy that was the release of the soul. The Cyrenaics adopted this crass form of radical indulgence in drunkenness and sex.

Epicureans: The Art of Finding Pleasure

The Epicureans of antiquity represented the second stage of hedonism. They were more sophisticated. Today we often use the term *epicurean* to describe a person with exquisite taste, one who can identify the finest wines, but who is not himself a drunkard. He has a gourmet palate and understands the intricacies of the culinary arts. He is knowledgeable about the finest clothes and appreciates the finer things of life, a person who is devoted to his creature comforts because he seeks to enjoy life by pursuing a sophisticated level of pleasure.

The Epicureans adopted a more refined variety of hedonism. They did so because they learned early the problem with Cyrenaic hedonism, the problem of excess. This problem has been referred to as the "hedonistic paradox": if the hedonist fails to achieve the measure of pleasure he seeks, he experiences frustration. Frustration is painful. If we fail to find the pleasure we are seeking, the result is frustration and pain. The more we seek pleasure and the more we fail to achieve it, the more pain we introduce into our lives. On the other hand, if we achieve all the pleasure we seek we become sated and bored. Boredom is the counterpart of frustration; it is also painful to the pleasure seeker. Again, the paradox: If we achieve what we want, we lose; if we don't achieve what we are searching for, we lose. The result of hedonism is the exact opposite of its goal. Its only fruit is ultimate pain.

The Epicureans also understood the price tag of pleasure. Part of the hedonistic paradox is that the momentary enjoyment of pleasure may have painful consequences. The Epicureans understood that if you indulged in too much wine, the result would not be exquisite enjoyment of fine-tasting wine, but the awful hangover of the next day. Likewise, if you overindulged in sexual activities, the odds were greatly increased that you would add venereal disease to your future misery.

Overindulgence has its price. In our own kitchen we have several warning signs: "Those who overindulge, bulge!" "A second on the lips, a lifetime on the hips!" Recognizing the price paid for pleasure, the Epicureans tried to create a more balanced enjoyment of pleasure and pain. For example, they believed that one should keep pleasure at a moderate level; just a little bit of adultery is enough to spice up life and keep the excitement flowing in the human heart.

Stoics: Seeking Peace of Mind

In addition, the Epicureans searched for the same thing that the Stoics sought, but they approached it in a completely different manner. The goal of Epicurean philosophy was the achievement of *peace of mind*. This quest was not unique to the Epicureans. Doesn't everyone want peace of mind? The answer is obvious, but how does one obtain it? The Stoics felt that the only way to find peace of mind was by adopting a philosophy they called "imperturbability." That means you don't let anything bother you. You adopt a "stoical attitude" toward all things. You do not get emotionally involved, you do not get your hopes up, nor do you let your hopes down, but you maintain an emotional state of equilibrium where nothing bothers you. You adopt a detached feeling toward those things over which you have no control.

This philosophy was based on a very deterministic understanding of the world. That is to say, all things happen by fixed mechanical causes. According to the Stoics, we cannot change things. *"Que será, será"* ("whatever will be, will be") was originally the song of the Stoics. They said, "The only thing that I have control over in my life is how I inwardly react to circumstance. If I'm going to get hit by a car this afternoon, I can't help that because I have no control over it." The Stoic sought to master the ability of being "cool." He would try to not allow anything to shake him up inwardly.

The Epicureans approached the search for peace of mind from the other direction. They believed that one could change the state of affairs as well as the events that affect our lives. That happens, primarily, through an active pursuit of pleasure and an active avoidance of pain.

Few people in our society will come right out and say, "Hedonism is my philosophy of life. I live for pleasure and for the avoidance of pain." Hugh Hefner of *Playboy* might put his name to a philosophy like this, but most people still have a negative opinion of this view of reality (even though we live in a secular environment). Yet in the same breath, we would all acknowledge that there is a little of the hedonist in every one of us. Even the masochist is a hedonist. He is a reverse hedonist, for he seeks to maximize pain, not in order to avoid pleasure but to gain it. He has a short circuit in terms of pain and pleasure, but he is still seeking pleasure.

In facing reality we need to ask ourselves, "Who does not want to have experiences that are pleasant?" Who really wants to enjoy pain? I'll be the first to admit that I want pleasure and that I want to avoid pain; I want comfort and I want to have a full stomach at the end of the day. I want to feel good; I don't want to feel bad! No one I know differs in that way. Hedonism has capitalized on a universal "given" in human nature. All persons are creatures of sensation. We have feelings. We experience pain and we don't like it. We experience pleasure and we do like it. What the hedonist does is to affix the suffix *ism* which transforms pleasure into a philosophy of ultimates. Pleasure becomes the ultimate criterion of value, so that truth and goodness are determined by what produces pleasure.

The Bible presents a very different view. Christ tells us from the beginning that a committed relationship with Him will involve pain. Christ was not a hedonist when He went up to Jerusalem. He had a duty to perform which was good and true, but which was also painful. The hedonists would declare Christ a fool forever. In their eyes, He voluntarily accepted unnecessary pain.

The Optimum of Pleasure Is in God's Kingdom

To put things in balance, we must say that Christianity does not call us to *seek* suffering, or to *pursue* pain, or to flee from that which is pleasant. There is no sin in enjoying the pleasant and being free from pain, but there are times when the Christian must choose the road that results in pain. Because of this, we do not consider hedonism as the highest good. We believe that the ultimate good will bring us the maximum pleasure and the minimum of pain. From a Christian perspective, the location of maximum pain is in the pit of hell and the optimum abode of pleasure is in the kingdom of God.

Pleasure is defined differently by the Christian than by the hedonist. Hedonism tends to see pleasure strictly on the level of sensual feeling, and it is restricted to physically quantifiable dimensions.

Try an exercise for the next week. Count the number of times you see or hear the word *feel* or *feelings*. Then consider how the word *feeling* functions in our culture. The term is so pervasive in our society that traditional forms of language have changed to accommodate it.

As a teacher, I read many students' papers. I wear out red pencils, not to mention my hand, correcting presentations that repeatedly say, "I *feel* that we should do this. . . ." "I *feel* that Descartes is wrong," or "I *feel* that Kant made a mistake here." The refrain is monotonous: "I feel, I feel, I feel." When the student declares, "I feel that Kant made a mistake" he means that he thinks Kant committed an error. The student is making a *cognitive* judgment. It is not a feeling, it is thinking. To be sure, thoughts evoke feelings. The student may feel remorse or jubilation about discovering an error in Kant, but that is a result of his cognitive evaluation. It is not the cognitive evaluation itself.

The exploration of feelings is appropriate for the physician or the psychologist. When an individual comes to me for counseling, I know that feelings are important. In such a situation, I don't ask the husband, "What do you *think* of your wife?" I ask *feeling* questions because I know they are the loaded ones where the emotions are expressed. I will ask him, "How do you feel when she does this or that?" I am trying to get at the feelings. I don't want to deny for a moment that feelings are an essential part of what it means to be human. But feelings are not the same thing as thinking. The sensuous has become so exaggerated in our culture that we talk about "feeling" ideas instead of "thinking" ideas, about "feeling" thoughts instead of "thinking" thoughts.

The interest of the general public in the relatively new science of psychology has grown at an explosive rate. We are a nation preoccupied with analyzing our moods and our feelings. One obvious manifestation of this preoccupation with feelings is seen in the explosion of drug use. Mind-altering drugs are used to induce euphoria. The cocaine and marijuana industries in this nation, as well as that of alcohol, are multibillion-dollar-a-year businesses.

In 1963 I was working at the Saint Francis Hospital in Pittsburgh. I remember one day a Cadillac limousine drove up in front of the hospital and a girl stepped out of it and was escorted to the psychiatric ward. She was admitted to the alcoholic section there. She was fifteen years old. The story of her admission went through the hospital like wildfire. It was astonishing to the workers that a fifteen-year-old girl could be a hard-core alcoholic. That was more than twenty years ago. Today there are literally millions of teenage alcoholics in the United States. The public broadcasting networks have sponored a film entitled *The Chemical People* that documents the epidemic spread of child alcohol and drug addiction. The quest for euphoria, for free-floating escape from pain has a heavy price tag.

"If It Feels Good, Is It Good?"

Hedonism makes a value judgment by saying that the avoidance of pain and the pursuit of pleasure are good. At the same time, it produces a system of ethics which, in turn, produces a certain behavioral pattern of morality. A popular maxim of our culture is "If it feels good, it is good." Goodness is determined by feeling. Popular music communicates the message that the final test of what is right is the feeling test.

The sexual revolution is rooted in a hedonistic ethic. A recent quote from author Helen Gurley Brown indicates how much our society has been influenced by hedonism. She has given us a new definition of promiscuity. In the fifties the word *promiscuity* meant "having sexual relationships with more than one person, outside of marriage." The new definition by Helen Gurley Brown is "Having sexual relationships with more than one person *in the same day.*" Catch that phrase, *"in the same day."* That is the new definition of promiscuity. We must understand that the sexual revolution our nation has experienced has not happened in a vacuum. There are cultural and philosophical reasons for these changes.

At the root, hedonism is a philosophy of despair. It reflects a deep-seated sense of hopelessness of people trapped on this side of the wall. It is a quasi-logical conclusion to secularism. If my life is bound by the poles of birth and death, if my life has no eternal significance, then why not grab whatever pleasure I can squeeze out of my brief time on earth? If death is ultimate and life is meaningless, we need an escape. Temporary euphoria seems better than none at all. The cocaine high, the sexual orgasm, the gourmet meal all offer at least a brief respite from constant despair. The final creed of the hedonist is "Eat, drink, and be merry, for tomorrow we die."

The ancient Epicurean and the modern hedonist both search for the same thing—peace of mind. They are looking for relief that goes beyond Rolaids. Peace of mind, however, is elusive. The deepest desire of man is for a stable peace, a peace that lasts without giving way to a hangover.

Saint Augustine was a crass hedonist before his conversion to Christianity. He pursued the sensuous route; he was a pleasure seeker. His famous prayer, penned after his conversion, expressed the human dilemma: "O God, thou hast created us for Thyself, and our hearts are restless until they find their rest in Thee."

Augustine saw a link between human restlessness, a gnawing form of anxiety, and living against the purpose of our creation. We were created for God. Just as fish are in despair out of water, so the human soul is in despair when it is outside of fellowship with God. The Westminster Catechism asks: "What is man's chief end?" The answer provided is: "Man's chief end is to glorify God and to enjoy Him forever."

The goal of man is God. He is the fountain of peace, the wellspring of joy. We were created for happiness, not gloom. We were created for hope, not despair.

Americans are guaranteed the "inalienable right to the

pursuit of happiness." There is a profound difference, however, between pursuing happiness and seeking pleasure. We often confuse them.

Sin destroys happiness. By sinning we violate God. We injure our relationship with Him. We frustrate the goal of our own humanity. But sin is pleasurable. If sin offered no pleasure it would have little attraction for us. The enticement of sin is for the short-term feeling of pleasure. Pleasure is so called because it is pleasing to us. It is pleasant. Happiness is also pleasant. It is also pleasing to us. We can state it this way: All happiness is pleasurable, but not all pleasure yields happiness.

Pleasure and happiness are closely linked. But happiness is a particular type of pleasure. It endures. It goes beyond momentary euphoria to blessedness. It yields the authentic fruit of joy, a joy that lasts forever.

Questions for Discussion

1. How do you describe a modern epicurean?

2. What is the hedonistic paradox?

3. What do you do to escape pain?

4. What do you do to seek pleasure?

5. How do you respond to the explosive use of drugs in our culture?

6. Why are teenagers becoming alcoholics?

7. What is the *Playboy* philosophy?

8. What is the difference between feeling and thinking?

9. What is the difference between pleasure and happiness?

10. What does the Bible mean by God's "good pleasure"?

Part II

The Christian's Role in Society

Chapter Nine

The Christian and World Economics: A Look at the Law and the Profits

Now THAT WE have considered various world views affecting American culture, I want to turn our attention to several aspects of our society to see how they are influenced by these world views. The specific aspects we will look at are science, government, literature, art, and economics.

For a Christian to be concerned about economics may seem, at first glance, mundane and worldly. Many Christians spend very little time considering the issues that are involved in economics, yet we are all aware of the contemporary situation of our society. Newspaper headlines and front-page stories now deal with aspects of economics. In the past it was normal to read about economics on the business pages of the paper. Now, however, presidential and congressional elections hinge on questions of economic policy.

Economic problems are not limited to the United States, but are worldwide in scope. We have been told by the sociologists and historians that, as a result of modern communications, our planet has become a "global village." What happens in Afghanistan is read about at the breakfast table the next morning in America. What happens in India affects the marketplace in Indonesia which, in turn, affects the United States. Serious worldwide inflation exists, and we are deeply concerned about it. At a personal level, this affects our material well-being.

As Christians, we are called to be profoundly concerned with ethics. The point that is often overlooked is that economics touches heavily upon ethics. Every time we choose to spend a dollar, invest a dollar, or save a dollar, we make an economic decision based on a policy that embraces ethics. When economic policy is legislated by a government, ethical decisions are being made. Why? Because economics has to do with monetary systems and the means of exchange within a given culture. Here we are immediately dealing with the question of value, and value is an ethical matter.

Oikonomia is the Greek word from which the English word *economy* or *economics* is derived. In the New Testament the word *oikonomia* appears frequently, but it is not translated as "economy" or "economics." It is translated "stewardship." Christians may not be deeply concerned about economics, but the New Testament certainly is concerned about stewardship. We see the concept on page after page. *Stewardship* comes from a combination of two words: *oika* which comes from the Greek word for "house," and *nomos* which comes from the Greek word for "law." *Oikonomia* has to do with "house law" or "house rule." The biblical idea is that the steward is the one who is placed in a position of authority over the house. The steward does not own the house, but he works for the owner and is given authority to manage the house.

Ultimately, the global house, biblically speaking, is the world, which is our home. God is the One who ultimately owns the world and man is placed in this world as a steward of God's house. Economics, therefore, has to do with managing the resources that ultimately belong to God. God holds us accountable for what we do in that management process as we take care of the world that He has given us.

Recently, I spoke on two parables from the Gospel of Luke. One was the Parable of the Prodigal Son and the other, the Parable of the Unjust Steward. Each has different points and different concerns but there is one interesting parallel. The prodigal son, after he received his inheritance, wasted his substance, while the unjust steward was dismissed by his employer because he wasted the goods of the owner of the house. In both parables, we see the negative judgment of God falling upon waste. To waste one's substance is an economic problem.

When we go to the Bible, we find allusions such as these to economic issues. The Bible is not a technical textbook on economic theory. It does not present a detailed blueprint for economic policy. That is not the purpose of the Bible. As a result, some Christians have concluded that the Bible is irrelevant to economics. But that is a perilous conclusion, as perilous as it is erroneous. The Bible sets forth vitally important ethical principles that have weighty significance for economic policy and decision making.

Let me outline four principles that are clearly set forth in Scripture. There are more principles touching on economics than these four, but these are ones that are repeated again and again. They are basic and foundational Christian principles of economics. These are our 1) private property, 2) equity, 3) industry, and 4) compassion.

Private Property

It is a popular practice for competing schools of economic thought to appeal to the Bible for support in order to gain an authority base for their programs. Communism, for example, points to illustrations in the book of Acts where, in the early church, people held things in common. Those who are advocates of communism (not in the Marxist sense) viewed communal living as beneficial and they appealed to the Bible as the platform for their economic policies.

Socialism seeks as its premiere goal the equality of wealth and equality of ownership within a society. To accomplish this, the government must be involved in the redistribution of wealth. Historically, socialism has been very concerned with the plight of poor people and oppressed people. Compassion has been the motivation for most varieties of socialism. The people have desired to redress the wrongs, the inequities, and the injustices that have been perpetrated against the poor. The Bible illustrates a concern for the material well-being of the poor and calls us to redress economic inequities. It also calls us to manifest compassion. We can see how certain strands of the Bible have become important to socialist economic theory and how certain aspects of biblical ethics are incorporated into it.

Capitalism has been historically linked with Christian theology, particularly with Protestant theology, and its emphasis on the so-called work ethic. The Bible does issue a strong call to industry. It has also been appealed to in order to support the primary principle of capitalism, which is private ownership. Does the Bible advocate private property? We have seen that the whole world belongs to God and we are His stewards, so, in the ultimate sense, we do not own anything. But in a sense, if we speak in terms of daily living on this planet, God does set forth principles of private ownership. He protects the rights of private property in the Bible. Consider two of the Ten Commandments: "Thou shalt not steal," and, "Thou shalt not covet." Both commandments presuppose private property.

Why, then, do these conflicting economic systems all appeal to the Scriptures for support? Part of the reason is that these four principles have some central importance in Scripture. The capitalist places his emphasis on private property, but private property embarrasses the socialist and the communist. Equality embarrasses the capitalist, but is very important for the socialist. Everybody claims to be industrious and everybody wants to be compassionate.

Equity

If I were to choose any one of these four principles and say that it is most central to the biblical concern for economics, I would choose equity. My second choice would be compassion. The Bible again and again reduces the essence of godly behavior to two virtues: justice and mercy. It is very easy to set justice and mercy over against each other, but the Bible refuses to do that. We are called to work for justice and we are also called to work for mercy.

Socialism destroys the equity principle and substitutes in its place a principle that sounds like equity but is not. Instead of equity, socialism presents the concept of egalitarianism in which the goal is to equally distribute the wealth of a society. This would be a noble thing, a marvelous ideal to hope for worldwide participation in the equal distribution of the enormous riches and wealth that this world affords. The problem that socialism fails to consider fully is that we live in a fallen world. In such a world, inequalities will inevitably exist with respect to personal wealth because some people will be more responsible than others. Equity with respect to justice requires that the responsible person not be penalized for being responsible and that the slothful person not be rewarded for his slothfulness. If we have a great leveling process where we take from those who are productive and gratuitously assign it to those who are not, we violate biblical principles of justice. If we do that in the name of compassion, we have a one-sided view of compassion. To steal from one man to give to another shows neither justice nor compassion for the victim of theft.

Industry

The Bible presents a strong work ethic that calls us to industry, to production, and to labor. God sanctifies labor. It is important to remember that labor does not come to us as a result of the Fall. It originates from our God who is a working God. God creates through divine industry, and He calls us to mirror and reflect that operation. God assigned labor to man before the Fall. He did not merely put man in a garden of paradise and say to rest for seven days a week. Adam was called to dress, till, and cultivate that garden. He was called to multiply. In other words, he was called to be *productive.* Integral to our vocations as human beings is God's design for us to be productive, to bring forth the fruit of our labor.

According to biblical principle, we are to be able to participate in the ownership of what we produce. The system of law that we find in the Old Testament is designed to protect private property from theft, fraud, and deceit. Numerous laws in the Old Testament are set forth to insure honesty in the business world and in the marketplace. It is unlawful, according to God, to defraud another by use of false weights and measures, to debase the currency of a society, or to renege on contractual promises and obligations. Related to these are the breaking of covenants and of industrial contracts Equity, with respect to industry, is an important principle of economics. Justice must be done.

The Importance of Compassion

What do we do with those who lack the means or the opportunity for production? Do we close our hearts to the poor? God forbid. God has a special concern for the poor. In the Old Testament law He demands that the fields be left at the corners to be gleaned by the poor. Laws are given by God to make sure that the poor are not ignored. Most importantly, the poor are not to be discriminated against at "the gates," which were the law courts of the land. The poor were not to be exploited or demeaned by the rich and powerful. The Bible also warns a person of the consequences of making the acquisition of riches the supreme goal of his life. The Bible says no to a crass form of materialism and tells us that life is more than wealth.

On the other hand, the Bible also says no to a false spirituality which maintains that what happens to man's body or to man's material well-being is inconsequential. God has created a physical world. He has created people with souls who also have bodies. His redemption includes bodily redemption. God is concerned about shelter, about food, about clothing. The Bible does not provide an exercise in abstract spirituality.

Some of the biblical concerns expressed about righteousness, justice, and compassion are concerns that touch the economic situation of men, women and children. The term *poor* is used figuratively in some verses in the Bible to refer to those who are poor in spirit, but its primary use is to refer to those who are poor in material goods. The Apostle Paul, at the heart of his teaching, says, "If your enemy is hungry, feed him; if he's naked, clothe him." What is Paul saying here? He is saying, in the simplest way, God cares about your physical well-being. He cares that we have enough to eat; that we are protected from the elements; that we have clothes and a place to live. These are economic matters. In essence, man's material welfare is a major concern of God and therefore it must always be a major concern of God's people. The biblical ethic is one of stewardship. The principles of stewardship demand certain principles that capitalism also embraces. However, capitalism can be construed as a license for crass materialism with no consideration for the poor. Capitalism is based upon production of goods and services. How these goods and services are used *and* produced are matters of ethics.

Virtually every significant effort aimed at improving people's standard of living invented by socialistic or communistic theories of economics has failed miserably. A case in point is China. Since the communist revolution there in 1949, the production, the standard of living, and the per-capita income of the people of China have declined to levels worse than they were before the revolution. Taiwan, the free region of China, has 18 million people; mainland China has over 1 billion. Yet the per-capita income on Taiwan is five times higher than on mainland China. During the decade of the seventies, the 18 million people of Taiwan exported fifty times more goods than the 1 billion people from communist China. To be sure, recent trends in China show an upturn in industrial output due in large measure to a growing toleration of private agriculture and private merchants.

The Principle of Production

Without production we do not have the food to feed people, the clothes to clothe them or the houses to shelter them. It is simple. The single most important factor to increase the material well-being of people is production. The greater the quantity of things produced, the lower the cost per unit for those things. Within limits, the more that is produced, the better the standard of living.

Increased production can benefit the poor man the most because the goods he needs are then more accessible to him. If a nation produces 100 shirts, the price of shirts tends to be high—too expensive for the poor man. If a nation produces 1 billion shirts, the price of shirts tends to be low. This reflects the law of supply and demand. Increases in production lower prices. But what if the poor man has no money? What difference does it make to him if a shirt costs five dollars or a hundred dollars? Here is the difference. In a situation of high productivity, employment also rises. The greater production of shirts provides a better opportunity for the poor man to enter the work force and increase his standard of living. Even if he fails to find work his chances of getting a "free" shirt are better if there is a surplus of shirts. People tend to be more charitable with five-dollar shirts than with hundred-dollar shirts. The workers in the Salvation Army are keenly aware of that.

The Principle of Tools

A second important principle is highlighted when we ask, "What is the single most important ingredient for production?" Karl Marx understood the answer to this question. The single most important factor for increased production is *tools*. Why is it that a peasant in Colombia cannot produce as much food as a farmer in America? Is it because the American farmer is more intelligent or that he is physically stronger? No, it is because a man with mechanized tools can produce a hundred times more than a man with wooden implements. Tools are what have revolutionized the world in terms of the production of material goods. A hundred years ago, 80 percent of the population of the United States were farmers. Today, it is about 3 percent, and this 3 percent produces more food than the 80 percent of a hundred years ago could produce. Why? Because modern techniques of production are based upon modern tools. Tools are crucial to production. They are labor-saving devices. More goods can be produced with less effort.

The Principle of Capital

What is the single most important ingredient for tools? Capital. Money is what is needed. The big difference between the poor peasant in Colombia and the American farmer is that the peasant does not have the tools. Why doesn't he have the tools? It is not that the tools are not available; the tools are there. But the peasant does not have the money to buy them. It takes money to buy tools which, in turn, are converted into productivity to increase the standard of living in the world.

Why is this important to understand? Because this is the central point of attack in the modern world. A vocal minority have made sharp attacks against excess capital. By "excess capital" they mean investment capital. In the socialist dream, if we make more money than we need to live on, this excess is taken and distributed around. Immediately, the key ingredient for the whole process of increasing the well-being of man has been destroyed. Without surplus capital, there can be no increase of tools; without an increase of tools, there can be no production; without production, the whole welfare of man fails.

The Principle of Profit

Taking one step farther back, what is the one thing on which capital depends? The answer is called an obscene word by some. The word is *profit*. Profit is the goal of all economic exchange. We can theorize all we want and declare that profit is obscene or that profits are too high, but every time an economic transaction takes place where goods are exchanged, the goal in that exchange is profit. The goal is profit, whether it happens in a communist country or in a capitalist country. Every time we are involved in an economic transaction, we are looking for a profit. The very basis for commerce is profit.

Consider this scenario. A shoestore owner pays twenty-five dollars for a pair of shoes. He then sells the shoes for forty-five dollars. Who profits? Before I answer, let me point out that I have asked this question of many large groups of people. In every instance the vast majority have answered, "The shoestore owner." The answer is only half right. To be sure, the owner profits. But so does the customer: if the purchase is voluntary.

When I go to the store and buy a pair of shoes, what motivates me to buy that pair of shoes? It could be the price or that my feet are cold or because I want to look nice for the dance. An ironclad principle is that I will never, of my own will, pay more for that pair of shoes than that pair of shoes is worth to me. Every time we enter into an economic transaction we are looking for a profit. In my mind, I decide that I want those shoes more than I want the surplus money I have in my pocket. I have a surplus of money, but I don't have a surplus of shoes. On the other hand, the shoemaker has a surplus of shoes, but he doesn't have a surplus of steak; and he wants some steak. The only way he is going to get steak is to sell part of his surplus of shoes to me so he can make the money he needs to buy steak.

On the surface, in the above scenario it *seems* like only the storekeeper profits. That is because money is used in the exchange. As a medium of exchange money is less direct than bartering. When we state the scenario in different terms the audience answers differently. Consider this scenario.

One man is a shoemaker. He makes a hundred pairs of shoes. Another man is a cattle rancher. He has a freezer full of meat. The shoemaker has more shoes than he needs, but no meat (he doesn't want to eat shoe leather). The rancher has more meat than he can eat, but his feet are cold. The two men get together and make a deal. They barter, trading meat for shoes. Now who profits? It is obvious that both profit.

Man survives by the *division of labor*. From the earliest chapters of the Bible we find society based on a division of labor. Cain was a tiller of the soil while Abel raised livestock. They needed each other. Barter was always for *mutual profit*. Mutual profit is the motive for all the free trade, for all voluntary business transactions.

Remember this formula:

Material welfare depends upon production
Increased production depends upon tools
Tools depend upon surplus capital
Surplus capital depends upon profit

We can chart it.

Material welfare
Production
Tools
Surplus capital
Profit

If we attack profits we destroy the foundation of man's material welfare.

Biblical ethics sees two grave vices as threats to stewardship. They are covetousness and greed. Greed acts as the motivating force behind exploitation and waste. We tend to think of greed as the sin of the rich and coveting the sin of the poor. Yet these sins are found in both groups. No man is so rich that he is incapable of coveting another person's property. No man is so poor that he is incapable of waste.

In a free market, an "invisible hand" helps restrain some of these evils. If a man is a crass materialist, avidly pursuing riches out of greed, even his greed can work for the general welfare. How? Suppose a man makes a billion dollars. What can he do with it? He can't eat a billion dollars worth of food. He may hoard his money by putting it in the bank; society has a strong bank to assist other businesses. He can waste his money on self-gratifying extravagances. He can buy ten Rolls Royces, three Learjets, and have five plush condominiums in Florida. Who benefits? The automobile industry, the Learjet people, and the condominium builders. It takes people to make Rolls Royces, Learjets, and condominiums. Even in this man's opulence the division of labor is served.

Yet, what if the man is cantankerous enough to hide his money in the basement? He has just taken a billion dollars out of circulation, causing deflation. Now everyone else's dollar is worth proportionately more and the prices of goods decline.

The worst thing that can happen to the man's money is to have it taxed heavily by government. Why? Governments are not producers. They produce nothing. To be sure, they redistribute money, but at a terrible waste of administrative overhead. Government-controlled economics are notoriously less efficient in raising national standards of living than is the free marketplace of voluntary exchange of goods and services.

Christians must work for a free market regulated by just laws. They must oppose the debasing of currency, unjust levels of taxation, and bureaucratic waste.

Questions for Discussion

1. Is it true that the rich only get rich at the expense of the poor?

2. How does poverty breed poverty?

3. How do tariffs affect the national economy?

4. Should governments subsidize failing industries?

5. Why are economic issues ultimately ethical issues?

6. Name three ways to reduce a government deficit.

7. How do we use government for personal profit?

8. Is a graduated income tax just? Why, or why not?

9. What is inflation? What is "fiat currency"?

10. What is money? Upon what is it based?

Chapter Ten

The Christian and Science: How to Fuse Faith and the Atom

WHAT IS the Christian's role in the scientific enterprise? How do we as Christians live in a culture that has been shaped and influenced by the impact of scientific accomplishments?

Lest we slip into critical attitudes toward science, we must remember that science began with a mandate God gave in creation. God commanded Adam and Eve to have dominion over the earth and to subdue it. There is a sense in which man was created to conquer the universe in which he lives. The scientific enterprise is a part of that task. At the same time, certain restrictions and constraints are placed upon man in creation. We are called not only to be productive, but to dress, till, and keep the earth, and to replenish it. In the initial mandate for the scientific enterprise, there were governing sanctions. The scientific enterprise is to be under the authority of God and restrained by the law of God. Implicit in the mandate is the prohibition against the exploitation of natural resources, the raping of the world over which we have been given dominion.

For centuries, there were broad areas of cooperation between the church and the scientific community. They worked hand in hand. The vocation of the scientist was seen as a calling from God Himself. There was a kind of unity between the spiritual quest of man and the natural quest of science.

Increasingly, it seems, a break is developing between man's spiritual life and his natural or scientific life. Perhaps we still have not healed the wounds from the Galileo episode in the seventeenth century. In that drama, Galileo was condemned by the Catholic Church for his scientific activity, and his scientific work was banned. Only recently has that ban been removed. This act served to heighten a growing sense that there are two different realms, the realm of faith or religion, and the realm of reason or science. The tension between the two accelerated in the nineteenth and twentieth centuries and came to a head in the 1925 Scopes trial involving the issues of teaching evolution.

Galileo: What Really Happened?

The Galileo trial is generally regarded as a black eye for the church. The popular impression is that Galileo's plight was the result of blind conflict between dogma and fact, between faith and science. A closer scrutiny of the historic debate reveals that the scientists within the church were as hostile to Galileo's discoveries as were the bishops. Galileo challenged the "orthodoxy" of science as well as the church. It wasn't merely the bishops who refused to look through his telescope. His fellow scientists were equally reluctant to take a peek.

Though the facts of history show otherwise, the impression that has been passed down to us is that the church and the church alone was guilty of suppressing Galileo's discoveries. As a result, the church lost credibility and a growing rupture occurred between church and science, a rupture that is utterly foreign to biblical Christianity.

We often hear the assumption that if one is to be a Christian in our modern age, he must be something of an intellectual schizophrenic. He must somehow put his faith on one side of the room and his reason and scientific investigation on the other side, because the two are simply incompatible.

We have been considering throughout our study the dilemma that modern man faces with that wall which divides the metaphysical realm from the physical realm. This great watershed in Western civilization came with the criticism of Immanuel Kant. Kant maintained that our normal methods of knowing man never take us beyond the limits of this world and into the realm of God. The scientific method, therefore, is useful for the study of physics, but not for the study of metaphysics. It is useful for the study of nature, but not for the study of super-nature. The essence of Kant's critique was that God cannot be known by theoretical thought.

That was a watershed moment in Western history. Since then, multitudes of thinkers have succumbed to skepticism and have said that if we are to have any knowledge of God or any religious truth, that knowledge must be achieved not by reason or by scientific observations. We must conjure up a new way to get over that wall. This is done either through an existential experience or through mystical intuition. The result is that normal avenues of knowing are closed to the things of God.

However, not every Christian has rolled over and played dead at the feet of Immanuel Kant. As soon as we embrace the idea that God is only known mystically and that the world is only known scientifically, we create a kind of personal schizophrenia that is intolerable for the intelligent person. Therefore, as missionaries to our culture, we must deal with this problem.

Is Aquinas to Blame?

Many Protestant scholars venture earlier into church history and lay the blame for this division at the feet of Saint Thomas Aquinas. Among Protestant thinkers, there seems to be a kind of allergy to the work of Aquinas. Francis Schaeffer, for example, is one who would lay much of the blame for today's schizophrenic view on Aquinas. Schaeffer argued that the root of modern man's trauma lies in the separation that Aquinas made between the realms of *nature* and *grace*. The realm of nature is the daily arena of his visible world, the scientific inquiry. The realm of grace is the supernatural realm of God. If Aquinas did in fact separate nature and grace, then certainly Dr. Schaeffer would be correct in pointing the finger at Saint Thomas for causing a significant part of modern man's dilemma. I plead for Aquinas, that he was not guilty of the charge. Aquinas did everything in his power to *prevent* a separation of nature and grace. He labored tirelessly to combat the efforts of philosophers who were making such a separation. Let us briefly consider the historical background.

In Aquinas's day, the Christian world faced the greatest threat that it had seen in centuries. This threat did not come from existentialism or pragmatism or secularism. The threat to the church in the twelfth and thirteenth centuries was the rising tide of Islamic religion and philosophy. The Crusades had attempted to recapture the sacred places of traditional Christianity, which had fallen under the dominion of the Turks. Islam had made an enormous impact in the world and was now reaching into Western civilization.

The greatest philosophical thinkers of the Islamic world had combined Islamic religion with Aristotelian philosophy to produce a system which they called "integral Aristotelianism." The technical term is not important to remember but the emerging relationship it represented is important. The product of this thought became widespread during this time and it greatly affected Christians. The key idea was called by the Islamic philosophers "double truth." The concept of double truth was that a notion could be true in theology or religion and, at the same time, false in philosophy or science. A person was expected to go through life holding both views which were, in fact, contradictory. In the twentieth century, this notion of double truth is more widespread than in any other period of civilization, even though we do not call it by that term.

I can illustrate the idea this way: on Monday, Tuesday, Wednesday, Thursday, Friday, and Saturday, I may say that I believe in chance evolution with no rhyme nor reason for it. Evolution was merely a chaotic result of chance. However, on Sunday I may believe that man was created in the image of God. By faith, I believe that man has dignity and purpose; that he is rooted and grounded in an intelligent act of creation by an Eternal Being. The rest of the week I have to be an honest scientist and believe that man emerged as a cosmic accident. How can I hold those two views at the same time? I am not attempting to raise issues concerning the various viewpoints of evolution and creationism. My purpose is to show that a belief in the two extremes at the same time demands a kind of intellectual schizophrenia. The two viewpoints are utterly incompatible. Yet people today want to be spiritual, and at the same time they want to be scientific. How can we deal with this dilemma?

Aquinas addressed the problem by distinguishing between nature and grace. Notice that he merely distinguished between the two, he did not separate them. He distinguished between those things which could be learned through a study of nature and those things which could only be learned through a study of grace.

Here we face a subtle matter that is often missed even by acute thinkers. There is a subtle difference between a *distinction* and a *separation*. Though the difference is subtle, it is vastly important. It has been said that "A woman's prerogative is to change her mind." We might add to that the saying, "A theologian's prerogative is to make distinctions."

One of the most important distinctions we can make is the distinction between a distinction and a separation. The graph below illustrates.

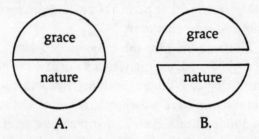

Figure A shows both nature and grace in the same circle. The parts of the circle are distinguished but the whole circle remains intact. The circle is unified. Figure B shows both a distinction and a separation. Here the circle is fractured and grace and nature are torn apart.

It is one thing to distinguish things; it is quite another thing to separate them. If I distinguish your body and your soul I do you no harm. If I separate your body and your soul, I murder you. If we distinguish the divine and human natures of Christ, we are orthodox; if we separate the divine and human natures of Christ, we are gross heretics.

When Aquinas distinguished between nature and grace, he said that we can learn certain truths only through the study of nature. We can study Scripture and pray all we want and we will not be able to discern the route that is taken by the blood in the human circulatory system. Nor will a close scrutiny of the Bible reveal all the intricacies involved in the Second Law of Thermodynamics or the process of an amoeba's split and growth. These things we learn through a study of nature. The Bible does not discuss every aspect of knowledge that is available to us.

Aquinas also said that certain things can only be learned by grace, by special revelation. We can study the circulatory system of the body, geometry tables, or any other scientific discipline but we will never discern in them the doctrine of the incarnation of Christ. Through a study of nature, we will never learn of the Atonement of Jesus or the sacrament of the Lord's Supper. Such information comes to us from God in Scripture.

All Truth Meets at the Top

Aquinas then insisted that there are "mixed articles," truths that can be learned from both nature and revelation. An example of a mixed article would be the knowledge that God exists. Aquinas was not separating nature and grace; he was showing us that both nature and grace ultimately lead us to the same place, to God. A study of nature may not teach us everything there is to know about God, but a correct study of nature will certainly teach us that there is a God.

Aquinas was an apostle of the unity of truth. His working assumption was that *all truth meets at the top.* What is true in science will ultimately undergird that which is true in religion. He is not saying that contradictions will be resolved at the top. He is saying that truth is always consistent and coherent. We may have in the Bible one source of information about reality, and in nature another source of information about reality. The Bible may provide information that is not obtainable from nature and, vice versa, nature may supply data which we have no knowledge of from the Bible. But those two sources of information can never conflict with each other if, indeed, we understand them aright. Does that mean that Aquinas therefore subordinated the Bible to science? Not at all. He affirmed that the highest source of truth is God's divine revelation in the Scriptures.

Yet the Bible is not the only source of revelation. There is that which we call "general revelation," and it comes to us from nature. The Bible itself speaks of it. What is known from nature can supplement what is known from the Bible. It can never contradict it. What do we do, however, if sometimes nature *seems* to contradict the Bible? This was the crucial problem in the case of Galileo. Galileo said, "I can prove that the earth is not in the center of the solar system by means of my telescope. Before now, we were unable to examine this with the eye, but now we can." Galileo said to the princes of the church, "Look through this telescope and see if I'm not right." The church leaders refused to look because they had already set in concrete a dogma that said that the earth was the center of the solar system. The princes said, "We don't care what the telescope says. You must be wrong because the Bible says that the earth is the center."

If the Bible teaches unequivocably that the earth is the center of the universe, then the center of the universe is the earth. However, we must first examine the Scriptures to see if God indeed says that. If there is absolutely no doubt that God says the earth is the center, then we know that the earth is the center of the universe regardless of what Galileo says. We can applaud to a certain degree the obstinacy of the church leaders because they were convinced that God had said one thing and they heard Galileo say another.

But the Bible does not say that the earth is the center of

the universe. The debate was not between God and Galileo, as the Catholic princes insisted; it was between the Ptolemaic astronomers and the Copernican astronomers. Unfortunately, the church rulers had put its blessing upon an earlier scientific model that they should not have blessed. They got egg on their faces when they tied the Ptolemaic system with divine revelation and eventually had to confess that they were wrong. In the final analysis, it was not a conflict between the Word of God and the word of Galileo. It is quite possible for science to correct theology. Understand—it is impossible for science to correct the Word of God, but it is possible for science to correct the word of the theologian. The judicious theologian must be careful to examine knowledge that comes to us from nature as well as knowledge that comes to us from grace, lest in a misguided zeal he establishes false conflicts between the two.

Historically, an example of a healthy attitude toward science and revelation was found in Isaac Newton. He did not live in fear of contradicting his faith through the study of the world. He said that the activity of the scientist is to think God's thoughts after him. Newton's was a humble, as well as a careful approach. He understood that all truth meets at the top.

Christians Need Not Fear Scientific Inquiry

There is a sense in which the Christian should be the most passionate scientist of all because he should be rigorously open to truth wherever it is found. He should not be afraid that a new discovery of something that is true will destroy his foundation for truth. If our foundation for truth is true, all other truth can only support it and enhance it. It can't destroy it. Therefore, Christians ought not to be afraid of scientific inquiry. This does not mean that we should uncritically accept all pronouncements and pontifications of scientists. Scientists are fallible and may occasionally make arrogant statements that go far beyond the realm of their own expertise.

Recently I read an essay by a well-known Nobel Prize winning physicist (whose name will remain unstated so as not to embarrass him) who argued that the idea of "spontaneous generation" be abandoned in science once and for all. Spontaneous generation means that something comes into being with no cause. It comes from nothing. So far, so good. I was pleased to see a scientist debunk the myth of all myths, that something can come from nothing. This myth is still pervasive in the scientific community with respect to "chance." Chance is given credit for creating the universe. However, such a prodigious feat is beyond the capabilities of chance. Why? Chance can do *nothing* because it *is nothing*. Chance is merely a word we use to explain mathematical possibilities. It is *no thing*. It has *no power*. It cannot produce, manage, or cause anything because it is nothing. It is spontaneous generation by another name.

I was glad the physicist repudiated spontaneous generation. My gladness abruptly turned to astonishment when the scientist said, "We must have a new model. We must speak in terms of *gradual spontaneous* generation." I couldn't believe what I was reading. "Gradual spontaneous generation"? How can something gradual be spontaneous? How can something spontaneous be gradual?

Our scientist wanted to debunk the myth that something can come *suddenly* from nothing and replace it with a better myth that something can come *gradually* from nothing.

I use this illustration only to show that even the most astute scientists can nod. They can fall asleep at the switch and be suddenly very unscientific in their pronouncements. To believe in gradual spontaneous generation of anything is to leap not by faith but below faith to credulity. Such a concept defies both aspects of the scientific method: rational deduction and empirical observation. Not only is the idea in violation of reason (breaking the Law of Contradiction), but it is impossible to observe empirically. What microscope or telescope is strong enough to observe anything doing something gradually spontaneously?

Occasionally, we read an article about why a certain scientist believes in God or why some other scientist does not. I am delighted when a scientist says that he has studied his area of science and is driven to the awesome majesty of God. But he is no more an expert on the existence of God than you are. Why? Because that is a theological question, not a scientific one. Today when somebody steps outside of his area of expertise, people tend to follow and believe him. That is the basis of much advertising. For example, a baseball star may appear on television and promote a particular brand of razors. If that star were to tell me how to hit a baseball, he would be speaking with authority. But when he tells me the best razor blade to buy is a certain brand, then he is speaking outside of his area of expertise. Advertisers understand that most people will easily transfer a person's authority in one sphere to other spheres. Scientists may be guilty of this fallacy too. We must be wary of scientists who make theological statements outside the boundaries of their discipline.

Our Age Cries for Talented Christian Scientists!

Another important consideration is an assumption that concerns the scientific method. The scientific method of inquiry is based upon a combination of two elements of knowledge: induction and deduction. Induction involves observing, measuring, and checking out particulars. Deduction involves applying formal laws of logic and coherency to those particular pieces that have been found. Both elements are needed in seeking truth. Some people are strong at induction and weak at deduction. Others are strong at deduction but are a little short on their research, experimentation or observation.

Christian science is, in the fullest sense, the responsible, sober, careful, humble investigation of truth using both induction and deduction, yet assuming at all times Aquinas's principle that truth meets at the top. Our age cries for talented scientists who see the scientific inquiry as a true vocation and as a response to the mandate of God Himself. Rather than flee from the scientific enterprise or embrace intellectual schizophrenia which only destroys, Christians are needed by the thousands to venture into the realm of nature, armed with the knowledge of grace. We can show that a God who exists on the other side of the wall is concerned with life on this side of that wall.

When we oversimplify theology or oversimplify science we encounter many difficulties between the two. Science is a complex enterprise. So is theology. Their relationship is to be studied closely and deeply if we are to discover an ultimate harmony between them.

One of my all-time favorite anecdotes concerns the meeting of a theologian and an astronomer. The astronomer was frustrated with the theologian for making religion too complicated. He said, "Why are you fellows so obscure? You talk about supralapsarian this and traducianism that. You quibble over fine points of predestination and God's omniscience. For me religion is simple; it's the Golden Rule: Do unto others as you would have them do unto you."

"I understand your frustration," replied the theologian. "You astronomers often confuse me with your talk of expanding universes this and exploding novae that. You're always talking about astronomical perturbations and galactic anomalies. For me astronomy is simple: It's twinkle, twinkle little star."

Questions for Discussion

1. What is science?

2. What is the scientific method?

3. What is the difference between a distinction and a separation?

4. Where do you see intellectual schizophrenia at work?

5. What is a double truth?

6. Does nature ever contradict grace?

7. How are Christians being received in the scientific community?

8. What is chance? What can it do?

9. Where do religion and science conflict?

10. Can a Christian believe in evolution?

Chapter Eleven

The Christian and Art: Painting by the Numbers

I LIVED IN the city of Amsterdam during the 1960s. As I walked through the city, I recognized the names on many of the street corners. There was Beethoven Straat, Vanderhelstlaan, and Rembrandt Plein. The streets and places that I encountered there often bore the name of famous composers or artists.

During my stay there I visited the Rijks Museum, one of the finest art museums in the world. It was an overwhelming experience. The transcendent beauty of painting after painting produced by the great masters of the history of art was inspiring. Many of these artists were dedicated Christians working in the world of art. The more I saw, the more I concluded that the golden age of Christian art in Western civilization has long since passed.

Today, in the Christian community, there seems to be a negative attitude toward art. Many think that art is unworthy of a Christian, as if art were something worldly, an illegitimate enterprise for Christians. In this chapter on art, I want to examine briefly this pervasive and negative attitude toward the whole field of art in the evangelical world.

As Christians, we are to be concerned about three qualities: the good, the true, and the beautiful. These three are virtues that touch the very heart of Christianity. It is a triad of values, each of which points beyond itself to the character of God. We are concerned about goodness because God is Good. We care about truth because God is Truth. We care about beauty because God is Beautiful.

When we study that which is good, we are concerned with ethics. When we study that which is true, we look into the arena of philosophy or epistemology. When we study the beautiful, we are dealing with aesthetics. If we look at the virtues of the good, the true, and the beautiful from a biblical perspective, certain principles leap from the pages of the Bible, which directly or indirectly deal with the concepts of beauty and of art.

The beginning of art is found in the act of creation itself. The ultimate foundation and basis for aesthetics is the work of creation. Here we encounter God the supreme artist. We are all aware of the beauty that surrounds us in creation. We rhapsodize about sunsets and about the Painted Desert in Arizona. We talk about a breathtaking panorama as we look from a mountaintop and see the display of beauty beneath us. These vistas of creation bear witness to the artistic virtue of God Himself. The psalmist says, "The heavens declare the glory of God; and the firmament sheweth his handywork" (Psalms 19:1).

Not only is God a painter, but He is also a craftsman. His work is extolled in the Scriptures for the creation of human personality. We are told that we are "fearfully and wonderfully made" (Psalms 139:14). Even in describing redemption, the New Testament borrows images from art. The Christian is said to be the workmanship of Christ (Ephesians 2:10). Christ is the ultimate craftsman who molds and shapes what He wants to form in you as a Christian.

With these plain evidences of art in creation, again I ask, Why does a pervasive negative attitude exist toward art in the Christian world?

I remember visiting Cumberland, Maryland, several years ago for a golf tournament. I happened to be paired in that event with a man who was the television announcer for the Baltimore Orioles. As he was addressing the ball, preparing to start his backswing, he stepped away from the ball, looked at us and exclaimed, "Isn't this incredible!"

"What do you mean?" I asked.

He said, "Look at the colors here!" And he called our attention to the fact that, in the landscape of the surrounding mountains, there must have been thirty distinct shades of green and none of them clashed. I had never considered the fact that there were so many nuances of color, hues, and shades existing side by side. If I tried to match my wardrobe like that, I would certainly end up with mismatching and clashing colors. But when God creates nature, He does it with subtleness of shade and of hue and of texture that somehow never clashes and is never ugly.

There Was Nothing "Tacky" About the Temple

If we move from the realm of creation to the realm of biblical history, again we see dimensions of God's involvement in art. In the Old Testament, God ordained and commanded the building of the tabernacle and later of the temple. These were extravagant projects of art. By divine imperative, the children of Israel were commanded to bring their gold and silver, to melt them down, and to use them for adorning the vessels that would be a part of the holy place and of the holy of holies. The finest wood was brought from the distant mountains of Lebanon. They imported the perfect wood of the cedars to be used in the construction of the temple. Certain craftsmen, like Bezalel and Oholiab, were given charismatic gifts, special supernatural endowments by God, so that they could perform their artistic tasks of forming, shaping, and polishing the furniture and the utensils of the tabernacle (Exodus 31:6). God spent the energy of His Holy Spirit on an artistic enterprise. There was nothing "tacky" about the temple. It was a building whose excellence in every way called attention to the glory of the God whose house it was.

I remember when my father came back from World War II after being in military campaigns in northern Africa and in Italy. He was troubled by his experience in war-torn Rome and when he came home he talked at length about his ambivalent feelings. He said, "I saw street urchins, children without clothes, children with their bellies swollen from malnutrition begging for bread, children with lice crawling in their hair. And not far away, I saw the Vatican City with walls covered with gold. I couldn't put together the poverty of the people and the opulence of the Vatican." That contrast has always been a problem for many Christian people.

I think we do have a historical precedent for the excellence of a church building that is built to the glory of God. It can be a great witness. On the other hand, church buildings and the art that adorns them can be an exercise in human arrogance. They can simply be monuments in human pride.

Recently I picked up a book written by Franky Schaeffer, Francis Schaeffer's son. He wrote it as a young man reacting to the impulses within the Christian world concerning art. If you recall the history of the L'Abri Fellowship, for many years the head professor of art at the Free University of Amsterdam, Dr. H. R. Rookmaaker, made annual pilgrimages to L'Abri and was intimately involved in shaping the philosophy of Francis Schaeffer. Dr. Rookmaaker's desire was to bring about a reformation of Christian art and, obviously, Franky Schaeffer was nurtured in many hours of discussion with Dr. Rookmaaker. In reading this book, appropriately titled *Addicted to Mediocrity*, I feel the strains of an angry man expressing his reactions to the inadequacy of Christian art today. He is precisely correct when he says:

> Today Christian endeavor in the arts is typified by the contents of your local Christian book store, accessories, paraphernalia shop. For the coffee table, we have a set of praying hands made out of some sort of pressed muck. Christian posters are ready to adorn your walls with suitable Christian graffiti to sanctify them and make them a justifiable expense. Perhaps a little plastic cube with a mustard seed entombed to boost your understanding of faith. If this were not enough, a toothbrush with a Bible verse stamped on its plastic handle, and a comb with a Christian slogan or two impressed on it. On a flimsy rack are stacked a pile of records; you may choose them at random, blindfolded, for most of them will be the same idle rehash of acceptable spiritual slogans, endlessly recycled as pablum for the tone deaf, television softened brains of our present day Christian.

Franky Schaeffer is very forthright in his opinion of art in the Christian community today. Christians have accepted a level of art that is marked by superficiality; art has become plastic, it lacks depth and substance. This is what Schaeffer means by an endless "recycling of hash and of pablum." What I find in so-called Christian art today is that which is not only superficial and cheap—but what is also boring. The beautiful should never be boring.

Why is this? Who is to blame? We are. We are the ones who demand the kind of stuff that the bookstore owner puts on his shelves, because he knows what will sell. Quality is never cheap; in fact quality has a tendency to be appreciated by so few people that it is not profitable. So quality gives way to profit.

Recently I was in Ocala, Florida, for a preaching mission and when I walked into the minister's office, I did a double take at the painting I saw on the wall. I asked him, "Where did you get that? It's my favorite painting. I've never seen it hanging in anybody's home, let alone in a minister's study!"

Usually, when I walk into a minister's study I see the same boring pictures that are found in every Christian bookstore. But the painting in this man's study was a reproduction of the famous Rembrandt painting originally titled "Jeremiah Lamenting the Destruction of Jerusalem." It represents one of Rembrandt's finest efforts.

Rembrandt frequently used episodes from biblical history or biblical characters as subjects for his paintings. Other of his paintings include the "Descent from the Cross" and a portrait of the Apostle Paul. In the painting of Jeremiah, we see an elderly man in a posture of almost total despair. His head is in his hands, and he is leaning on a big old book which is the Word of God, the Bible. In the background are the faint images of a city being destroyed and of people fleeing for their lives. In the foreground, the prophet contemplates and laments the vision of the total annihilation of the Holy City.

The Fruitful Moment

Rembrandt used a fascinating technique whenever he painted his portraits, much like Michelangelo did when he created his sculptures. He used a technique later described by German philosophers (particularly Herder) as the "fruitful moment." (The German word for *moment* means "the blink of an eye.")

One of the problems that an artist must deal with is the question of how to capture the essence of a human personality in a single painting. Life is a process, it is dynamic. A sequence of many different events shapes and forms our lives.

For this painting, Rembrandt approached his work by reading the biblical account of Jeremiah. He immersed himself in the text of Scripture trying to gain a comprehensive understanding of the style and the movement of the life of the weeping prophet. He then got out his pad and began to sketch scenes. He sketched up to eighty scenes from the life of Jeremiah, all the while searching for that fruitful moment, that one moment in the life of the man that would, somehow, capture in freeze-frame the essence of his personality. In the painting of Jeremiah, one can see the pain etched into the lines on his forehead. The conflict between the light and the darkness that was so much a part of his life is evident. The disappointment and the frustration of the prophet are captured as his head has become too heavy for his neck to hold up. We can look at Rembrandt's painting a thousand times and see something in it that we never saw before.

Michelangelo had the same approach. After drawing many sketches, he chose to depict David with stones in his hand. As we look at that famous statue, there is that sense of readiness, as if David were ready to spring into action.

The substance, depth, and thought behind the works of the masters gave their art an enduring value that far transcends the cheap, the boring, and the superficial.

The same can be said of the music of the great musicians. Does Mozart's music ever go out of style? Does Chopin's music ever get boring? Does Handel's *Messiah* still move us when we hear the "Hallelujah Chorus"? Watch the national music charts each week as they record the most popular songs across the country. The songs rise and eventually fall in a matter of a few weeks. What was Number One this week may not be in the Top Forty six weeks later. Many of today's songs are there for a moment and then they are gone. Great art, on the other hand, has the ability to persevere through time.

What Is "Christian" Art?

But what makes art *Christian* art? Is it simply Christian artists painting biblical subjects like Jeremiah? Or, by attaching a halo, does that suddenly make something Christian art? Must the artist's subject be religious to be Christian? I don't think so. There is a certain sense in which art is its own justification. If art is *good* art, if it is *true* art, if it is *beautiful* art, then it is bearing witness to the Author of the good, the true, and the beautiful. I think it is wrong for Christians to demand of their artists that they paint only themes which are overtly and directly religious. There is nothing wrong with religious themes, but the theme does not have to be religious to be "Christian." In a sense, the subject matter of Christian art may be exactly the same as that of non-Christian art. The Christian's goal, however, is to seek to express and capture the beautiful, the good, and the true.

This leads to the last issue that I would briefly touch upon: whether or not Christians need to be careful with the *form* of their art and not simply its *content*. Some theorists argue that the form of art is utterly neutral and that it does not matter what form art takes as long as we are careful of the content. I disagree with this. I think a Christian may use many different forms in his painting, but we need to be aware that sometimes the *form* of a painting itself is a part of the message. When formlessness or the chaotic is the structure of the painting, that, in itself, is a statement that reality is ultimately chaotic.

As Christians in the realm of art, our impetus for producing Christian art is a desire for excellence. That desire stems from the fact that the God who has ordained this world is the supreme example of excellence in all that is good and true and beautiful.

If we are to produce a new generation of Christian artists, we must stop stabbing young artists in the back. We must stop accusing them of being "worldly" and "unspiritual." We must encourage Christian art—good art. Art is a form of communication. God Himself is a communicating God. He communicates to us both verbally and nonverbally. Our church services are marked by Word *and* sacrament. The sacrament contains forms of a nonverbal sort that communicate profoundly of God's redemption. If we cut off the aesthetic element from our triad of virtues we are left with a truncated Christianity and a God who at best is dull, and at worst, is ugly.

Questions for Discussion

1. How did God use art in the Old Testament?

2. How does art communicate?

3. What place does art have in the church?

4. What does church architecture communicate?

5. What is the nonverbal message of your church building?

6. How are clothes an art form? What messages do clothes give?

7. Why does today's Christian art tend to be tacky?

8. How do you think Jesus would respond to the products sold in Christian bookstores? Why?

9. How does form in art contribute to its message?

10. How do you define beauty?

Chapter Twelve

The Christian and Literature: Faith and Fiction

IN CERTAIN PERIODS of western history, Christian intellectuals have dominated the literary scene as they also did in art and music. But it is not true in any of these fields today. It is difficult to understand why this is so. Perhaps it is because there is a negative attitude among many Christians toward literature just as is the case toward art. For some reason, a strong prejudice against Christian involvement in these arts persists, except in a superficial way. Not only does literature suffer from a lack of appreciation among Christians; it suffers in general throughout our culture.

A recent report from the Center for Book Research at the University of Scranton revealed that less than 5 percent of Americans purchase books in a given year. I found this statistic shocking—but significant. What surprised me even more was that the current figure represents a major *increase* in per-capita book sales in the United States. Sales per capita rose from 2.75 in 1970 to 4.89 in 1980. The same period saw record growth in library usage.

Another significant statistic is found in the number of books published annually. In 1950, approximately eleven thousand different titles were published in the United States. That figure rose to forty thousand in 1975, and to fifty thousand in 1983.

Two factors must be noted here. Even with more books being published and increased library usage, those who actually buy books form a small fraction of the American public. For the business of publishing this means tough competition in the marketplace.

This competition reveals a second factor. In order to survive, a publisher or bookstore owner must appeal to the widest possible tastes among those few who do buy books. Frequently, the result is that what sells is not always what has the highest literary quality. Examine the *New York Times* best-seller list. Occasionally, but not often, do we find first-rate literary works there. Walk into a Christian bookstore and see what books have the highest sales. The plea of the publisher is, "Put the cookies on the lowest shelf." This is a publishing version of the KISS principle: "Keep it simple, stupid!" Simple books sell more widely than difficult books.

Writing simple books is itself an art. The line between being simple and being simplistic is all too easy to cross. Simple books on weighty subjects enhance Christian education. Simplistic books on weighty subjects obstruct Christian education. My guess is that in the current Christian bookstore the simplistic books outweigh the simple books by at least 10 to 1. I've often wondered where Jesus would apply His hastily made whip if He were to visit our culture. My guess is that it would not be money-changing tables in the temple that would feel His wrath, but the display racks in Christian bookstores.

I don't know where the burden of blame should be laid; with the publishers, the bookstores, or the customers? But

one thing is manifest: the Christian book industry is odorif-
erous.

Of course, it is difficult to survive in Christian publishing.
There is often conflict between mission and business reality. If a publisher or a bookstore owner is in business as a
vocation he experiences this conflict. He must sell books to
survive. He is faced with the same problem the secular
bookseller faces: trash sells.

I have published fifteen books with seven different publishers. In my contacts with those publishing houses, I have
found but two editors knowledgeable in theology, and no
more than three who were knowledgeable in literature.

J. I. Packer's *Knowing God* provided one of the greatest
surprises of recent Christian publishing when sales figures
climbed month after month. The Christian public aston-
ished the industry by revealing a deep interest in substan-
tive literature.

The Writer: a Verbal Artist

When we consider the topic of literature, of necessity we
need to ask, What is a writer? Our concern here will focus
on the novelist rather than the poet or the journalist. A
writer can be described as a verbal artist. The primary task
of the novelist is to produce works that are concrete rather
than abstract. There is a filtering process whereby abstract
ideas trickle down from the technical literature into the
more broadly read works. Through this process our values
and life views are influenced by the world of intellect.

In this filtering process from abstract to concrete, we can
see how those abstract ideas eventually reach the general
public. The normal pattern from theoretical concept to behavioral influence comes through an intermediate form of
communication that includes the novelist, the musician, and
the artist. If we examine the history of art or music or litera-

ture, we notice that the individual histories of these particular disciplines tend to follow parallel movements in philosophy. The rational period in philosophy produced the age of neoclassicism in music, literature, and art. Nineteenth-century thought produced the age of romanticism. Philosophy and the arts tend to walk arm in arm.

Claude Debussy, the French composer, wrote such famous works as "Claire de Lune" and "Prelude to the Afternoon of a Faun." His music had a different sound. His treatment of musical form and harmony helped change the direction of music in this century. Even today, his music sounds progressive. Debussy ackowledged that his music was greatly influenced by literature and painting. He did for music what Monet, Gauguin, Lautrec, and Van Gogh did for art. He implemented the philosophy of impressionism in the field of music. Debussy's work illustrates the relationship between philosophy and the intermediate level of art that helps to transfer philosophical ideas to a broader public. Eventually, the ideas filter down to the newspapers and the magazines to reach the level of the general population.

The fiction writer's work is similar to the work of the artist in the sense that his medium is nature. He finds his references in the real world. He uses concrete images to describe what is developing. I recently asked my editor at Harper and Row, "How do you go about writing a novel?" He told me, "You don't approach the writing of a novel in the same way you would if you were writing a textbook of theology or philosophy. You must write in concrete images, drawing from your own experience. You must paint word pictures. You must create an atmosphere and an environment. The writer uses vignettes from real life which do not merely imitate what is transpiring, but are also calling attention to people's feelings and experiences that either point them toward God or away from God."

By this means, concrete images of literature become symbols of that which is more abstract. The great literature of the ages is not written merely to imitate life. Great literature is written in the same way a great painting is painted. It is created to convey an understanding of something higher or deeper, captured in a brief moment.

I have previously noted the prevailing sense of the loss of transcendence in our culture. This is evident in the literature themes of our day. They differ from those of earlier days when the transcendence of God was still assumed. An example of this difference may be seen by comparing the works of John Updike in the twentieth century and the works of Herman Melville in the nineteenth.

"I Have Written a Wicked Book"

Melville has been described as America's greatest novelist. He wrote adventure novels, mainly about life on the high seas, as well as some short stories and poetry. His great classic is *Moby Dick*.

On the surface, *Moby Dick* is a novel of the search for a fierce white whale. Melville teaches the reader the techniques for hunting a whale—how to chart the waters, what ships to use and the correct hunting strategy, as well as the proper metal for harpoons. He even wrote chapters that laboriously describe how to melt down whale blubber. The detail of the book is extraordinary. While the novel appears to be about hunting whales, in reality it goes much deeper. The book is perhaps the most intensely theological novel ever written in America. When Melville completed the book, he wrote a personal letter to Nathaniel Hawthorne in which he said, "I have written a wicked book."

I have never read a chapter more moving, more poignant or more full of insight than the chapter titled "The Whiteness of the Whale." Here is pure literature in its classical sense. Read that chapter on your own. As you read, look for the symbolism in it. The whale is God. Notice how elusive the whale is. The whale is white. White is the color which symbolizes purity; yet it is a symbol as well for that which is threatening, frightening, and terrifying.

Moby Dick is the story of a man—Captain Ahab—who has one consuming obsession in life. Having lost a leg in a previous encounter with Moby Dick, now Ahab intends to capture the white whale and take out his revenge. He will pursue that whale, if need be, to the very depths of hell. Ahab travels across the world, giving up all of his other responsibilities in his mad pursuit to control, to plot the movements, to know every action of the white whale. On the symbolic level, Ahab is a man who seeks comprehensive knowledge of God in order to reduce God to something he can control and manipulate. *Moby Dick* is metaphysical; it is a novel of transcendence.

That we live in an age of the loss of transcendence might suggest that contemporary novels are not concerned about religion. Yet the contrary is the case. As secular as we are in society, we rarely pick up a novel today without finding some allusions to religion in it. It seems as though novelists are preoccupied with the question of the existence of God. The attitudes are different, the assumptions are different, and the feelings are different; but the authors all touch on the subject of religion. Often what we find in contemporary literature is a sense of the *absence* of God. There is a haunting feeling of loneliness. Authors similar to Nietzsche write of the death of God, but they do it with tears in their eyes. At the same time, we see other novelists who write with a guarded sense of hope, expressing the desire that there is a God who will somehow break in and make a difference in the future. As I mentioned previously, the play *Waiting for*

Godot expresses this perspective. In it, man is waiting for the appearance of God in history.

In much of modern literature there are also strains of bitterness toward religion and even overt hostility to the church. This anger may be expressed toward people who are religious and even toward God. When I say that novels are filled with allusions to religion, the allusions are not all positive, by any means. The point here is that religion is not ignored in modern literature. It's there. Virtually every book has a character who is a clergyman or someone with a religious fixation. The character is either maligned or people are trying to run from him. This is pervasive in contemporary writing. The modern novel shows what Calvin declared centuries ago, that man is incurably *homo religiosis*, "man the religious one."

Is John Updike a religious writer? His book *Rabbit Is Rich* won the Pulitzer Prize in 1982. He has written several novels as well as short stories and poetry. The book that catapulted him to national fame was the first of the Rabbit trilogy, *Rabbit Run*. Published in 1960, *Rabbit Run* was a poignant portrait of a young man growing up in a small Pennsylvania town going through all the trauma that a young man went through in that particular generation. Updike's literary skills were heralded.

His book, *Couples*, published in 1968, also became a bestseller, but it also scandalized the public. It was a New England version of *Peyton Place*, with graphic scenes of adulterous relationships sprinkled throughout the novel. It seems that with each novel, Updike has become more graphic. Yet Updike was consciously trying to write from a theological perspective. A voracious reader of theology, he attends a Congregational Church in Ipswich, Massachusetts. Updike reads Barth, Tillich, Niebuhr and de Chardin.

He has included much theological symbolism in his novels. Some people overlook it because of his graphic portrayal of the less cerebral dimensions of human life.

The novel is an art form. It is a unique vehicle of communication, going beyond recording life to interpreting it. The novelist is able to create a world and invite the reader to step into that world. He seeks to create a feeling of empathy for his characters. He wants the reader to care what happens to his characters. The reader is enabled to "get inside the heads" of the characters to peer at their innermost thoughts, to feel their visceral reactions. The novel must "work" first as a story before it can effectively convey a message.

Do Christians Read Novels?

Here is the point where Christian fiction faces a crisis. An impression that is rapidly being elevated to the level of an axiom is that "Christians don't go to movies or read novels." To the extent that is true is the extent to which the Christian community has surrendered these art forms to the pagan. Christian publishers invest little in fiction. What fiction is produced is usually romanticized portraits of biblical heroes or heroines, or fantasy novels. The so-called mainline novel is rarely found in Christian bookstores.

Why? Christians want their novels to preach the gospel. The message of Christ must be clear and forceful or the reader asks, "What is Christian about this?" The message must be loud and the characters perfectly spiritual. Any lapse into realism is seen as a betrayal of the gospel. Sin in the lives of Christian fictional characters must be concealed.

The message of such books gets across. The message the world hears is that Christians are phony. The world sees us as moralistic, judgmental, and preachy. Perhaps that is because we have used the novel as a dishonest form of preaching.

For a novel to work, the world depicted must be credible. That is true even in fantasy literature. There must be an authentic ring of truth in our writings. One need not be sleazy to be realistic, but one must be real. Realism demands that we be real. It is that simple. To be real means that we must stop lying in our literature. The world God created and is redeeming is a real world. Pollyanna is not a saint.

The novelist selects the dimensions of life that he is seeking to describe. In so doing, the writer must acquire something similar to the eye of the artist. He has to observe. He must also be able to see what is happening around him and then to translate that into verbal images that will create a picture for the reader to see.

A few years ago I decided to take lessons in sketching. After a few lessons, I noticed that I was viewing common things from new perspectives. As I drove my car from Stahlstown to Ligonier, the trees along the way that I had been passing for years suddenly appeared in a new and different light. I began to notice trees where I formerly observed only branches and leaves; I now began to see how the light was hitting a tree, and the texture of the bark. Suddenly I realized that, because of my art lessons, my eye was being trained to see things that I had previously overlooked. This is the skill that the novelist must develop. He must be able to see what others pass by and do not see. He can take the ordinary and the commonplace and make it extraordinary and significant.

When we lived in the Netherlands, a special exhibit was staged in the Stadelick Museum in Amsterdam featuring the very early charcoal sketches of Van Gogh. Van Gogh started out as a seminary student training for the ministry. As part of his internship, he was sent to minister to the poverty-sticken Flemish coal miners in Belgium and there he began to manifest his deep psychological problems of depression that led to his later dementia.

His earliest work consisted of sketching what he saw in the lives of the miners who lived in abject poverty. The exhibit featured numerous sketches of shoes. Van Gogh sketched the shoe of a Flemish coal miner with such intricate detail that the shoe told the story of the misery of these people. By sketching one shoe he was able to capture the life of the Flemish miner. In terms of the "fruitful moment," that one image of the shoe sketched in charcoal and showing all of its creases, its scuffs, its dirt and grime, spoke loudly. It was a statement about life. Van Gogh could not have made that statement if he had not first had the vision to recognize what was right in front of him. That is what a verbal artist is able to do with his writing.

The Problem for Christian Writers

Not long ago, I received a phone call from a Christian academy that was struggling with the problem of censorship. The parents of students were up in arms because their children were reading Steinbeck in the English classes. The school's dilemma was how to train people in American literature if they could not allow students to read Steinbeck. Steinbeck captured the plight of the American migrant worker and his problems as well as the theological significance of the situation in the same way that Van Gogh was able to capture the plight of the Flemish miners. Experts on Steinbeck insist that he included christological symbols and figures in his writing. The issue in question centers on how much realism can be portrayed if the writer is going to be accepted as Christian.

The Christian novelist faces the problem of how to be realistic without being crude. I faced this issue in writing *Stronger Than Steel*. At one point, I had to record a conversation that was pivotal to the conversion of Sam Piccolo. It happened during a drunken brawl in a motel. The dialogue was electric. How does the writer handle a situation in which a tough steelworker is ready to kill another man? A steelworker doesn't say, "Well, sir, I am about to dispose of your life." That's not the way he talks. But, if you say in print exactly what he said on that occasion, it's virtually pornographic. A writer who knows how to create literature can communicate what was actually said with the same force, and do so with a rich use of language in the same way Melville was able to.

Recently I received a letter from Pat Conroy, the author of *The Great Santini* and *The Lords of Discipline*. In writing my last book on human dignity, I was writing about problems in the work world. Particularly, I was discussing the importance of recognizing achievement on the job. Some receive a tangible expression of recognition such as a watch or plaque after twenty-five years of service. People will work hard to obtain some visible form of recognition that says, "You are important. You have dignity." At the time I was writing about that, I also happened to be reading *The Lords of Discipline*, which is basically a study of cadet life in a military academy, the Citadel.

Conroy describes the anguish and struggle and sacrifice required of the cadets in order to graduate and join the "long gray line." He describes the tradition and the symbolism that accompanies the ceremonies. When a cadet finally makes it through that four-year endurance race and graduates, he joins the ranks of those who have successfully gone before him. As a symbol of achievement, he is given his class ring, which becomes his greatest treasure. In most places a class ring is a nice memento, but the ring at that military academy meant everything and subsequently the men would give their all just to join the "order of the ring."

When I read that passage in Conroy, I thought it was magnificent! For many paragraphs he describes the significance of the ring. It is the closest thing that I have read to Melville's "The Whiteness of the Whale." At the time I discovered this, a friend of mine in Memphis was writing a novel and we were exchanging correspondence on his work. As we did so, I mentioned to him my excitement about Conroy's profound use of language and his ability to create verbal images. And I commended the reading of Conroy to him. My friend then wrote back and, over a period of time, we exchanged several interesting letters discussing Conroy's work. Later I thanked Conroy for his book and sent him copies of the correspondence, letting him eavesdrop on two other writers who were talking about him behind his back. I never expected to hear from him because I thought my letter would simply be one of thousands that a best-selling novelist would receive. But I received a handwritten letter from Conroy, who was then in Rome. The amazing statement in his letter was that he said how wonderful it was that a Christian liked his books. The rest of the letter went on to tell about the theological impulses that had affected his life and to ask for more correspondence about these things. He lamented the fact that, in Southern Baptist circles out of which he came, his literature had been completely dismissed as being the work of the devil.

The challenge for the Christian is to not join the legions of those who ignore the literature of his day. As missionaries to our culture, we need to support Christians who will make a serious contribution to the medium of literature, a contribution which will communicate with our culture and influence it for good.

Questions for Discussion

1. Where do you obtain the books that you read?

2. How many books do you read in a year?

3. Do you ever feel overwhelmed by the "present explosion"?

4. How do novels influence culture?

5. What makes a novel "Christian"?

6. How graphic and realistic is the Bible?

7. How do you respond to swearing in print?

8. Should books by Steinbeck and Hemingway be read in Christian schools?

9. How satisfied are you by the literature you find in Christian bookstores?

10. How is symbolism found in *Moby Dick*?

Chapter Thirteen

The Christian and Government: What to Do When Uncle Sam Wants You

AN AREA of controversy for many Christians is their relationship to the ruling government. Some think that the Christian, belonging to the kingdom of God, should have nothing to do with the powers and principalities of this world. Others declare that loyalty to nation and government is a prime responsibility of the Christian. What is to be our attitude and response to the government of our country?

One of the most important teachings we have in the New Testament to help us understand this relationship is found in Romans, chapter thirteen. There Paul sets forth the Christian's civil responsibilities. Some historians have declared that Romans 13 is the most important document in the political history of Western civilization.

The relevant text of Paul's instruction is as follows:

Let every soul be subject unto the higher powers. For there is no power but of God: the powers that be are ordained of God. Whosoever therefore resisteth the power, resisteth the ordinance of God: and they that resist shall receive to themselves damnation. For rulers are not a terror to good works, but to the evil. Wilt thou then not be afraid of the power? do that which is good, and thou shalt have praise of the same: For he is the minister of God to thee for good. But if thou do that which is evil, be afraid; for he beareth not the sword in vain: for he is the minister of God, a revenger to execute wrath upon him that doeth evil. Wherefore ye must needs be subject, not only for wrath, but also for conscience sake. For this cause pay ye tribute also: for they are God's ministers, attending continually upon this very thing. Render therefore to all their dues: tribute to whom tribute is due; custom to whom custom; fear to whom fear; honour to whom honour.

In this chapter I will feature for our instruction the chief principles set forth in the text. To simplify I will use a sequence of numbered articles.

1—All men are called to obey magisterial authority. The principle of obedience to earthly authorities is set forth as an integral element of our obedience to God. God alone has supreme authority over us. He alone can bind the conscience absolutely. As our supreme ruler, God has delegated authority to lesser powers and agencies. Our obedience to God must be reflected consistently by our obedience to His delegated authorities.

2—Governing authorities are ordained, instituted, and regulated by God. No man has rightful authority over other men which is not derived from God. All human authority is delegated and ministerial. This includes the authority of parents, bosses, policemen, dogcatchers, teachers or any other authority.

We note that the authorities that are to be obeyed are the powers "that be." That is, the question of how or why a ruler comes to power does not determine our responsibility to obey. Here the accent is on the *de facto* authority rather than *de jure* authority. We learn from this that human authority structures are contained within the broader structures of God's overarching providence.

It is important for us to discern the difference in the English language between the concept of power and the concept of authority, a distinction that is not immediately evident from the biblical text. The Bible speaks of authority by using the Greek word *exousia*. It is sometimes translated by the word *power*. What is in view is an authority that has power. Power naturally goes with authority, but authority does not always accompany power. For example, if we consider the local church structure we may find a ruling body such as a session that is endowed with judicial authority to govern the church. The elder has authority. Perhaps in the same congregation there is an individual whose contributions to the church equal half of the church's budget. Suppose that large donor is not a member of the session. The donor has no authority to govern. But he does have power. He has the power of influence and what we call "clout" because the threat of the loss of his monetary contribution can intimidate people. He has power, but no authority. In Romans 13, the call to obedience is to those who have actual authority, not to those who merely possess *de facto* power. There is a crucial difference between *de facto* power and *de facto* authority. It is authority that is in view here.

3—Resistance to divinely appointed authority results in divine judgment. Some translations of the text use the word *damnation.* This is an archaic translation of the Greek word for "judgment." In modern usage the word *damnation* suggests the ultimate judgment of the wicked to hell. Though illegitimate civil disobedience is a sin against God and is therefore worthy of eternal damnation (as all sins against God are so worthy), the ultimate penalty for sin is not what is specially in view in the text. Rather, we are warned that failure to obey the civil magistrates will result in our judgment at the hands of God.

The most frequently raised question at this point concerns the issue of the extent of our obedience to earthly authorities. Must we always obey the civil magistrate? Must students always obey their teachers? Employees their employers? Children their parents? The clear biblical answer to this is an emphatic no. There are times when we not only *may* but *must* disobey earthly authorities. Whenever the earthly authority commands us to do something that God forbids, or forbids us from doing something God commands, it is our duty to disobey the earthly authorities. God's authority is always higher than his delegated officers.

The fact that some acts of civil disobedience are necessary complicates the whole matter of obedience to authority. Some mistaken teachers insist that we are always and everywhere required to obey those in authority over us. This simplistic view would have people excuse themselves from atrocious crimes by appealing to the fact that their superiors commanded them.

On the other side of the ledger are those who think, since some acts of civil disobedience are permissible, that such activities can be engaged in for political reasons. We may not disobey authorities because we disagree with them or because their mandates inconvenience or even oppress us. The biblical principle is to render obedience wherever we can unless our doing so conflicts with our obeying God.

4—Government is instituted to promote justice. Paul calls the government a "minister" to us for good. It is not to be a terror to the good, but to the evil. Here the reference is to the legitimate design of government and not to its abuses. We know that governments can be demonized; they can be institutions of tyranny and oppression. When governments become unjust in their policies and practices it is particularly heinous because their primary purpose for existence is to promote justice and to protect the innocent from the machinations of the wicked. Saint Augustine said, "Without justice, what are kingdoms but great gangs of robbers?"

5—The state is endowed by God with the power of capital punishment. Government is force. The most basic ingredient that serves as the foundation for any state is the legal right of coercion. Without the right of forcible law enforcement (a redundancy made necessary by the overuse of the term *law enforcement*), the state can only make suggestions. Force is the legal means by which the state assures compliance to its laws. That force is symbolized by what Paul refers to as "the sword." God gives the power of the sword to the state. It is to be used to insure justice.

In antiquity the sword was more than a symbol of authority; it was a symbol of the right of life and death. The common method of capital punishment was decapitation by the sword. Paul indicates here the state's right to inflict punishment even unto death. (The irony is that it was this state's sword that ended Paul's own life.)

6—Obedience to civil authorities is a religious obligation. Paul calls us to subjection for "conscience' sake." That is to say that we are to render obedience to those in authority over us out of a regard and respect for God. His authority stands behind and above the lesser authorities of this world.

Our consciences are ultimately bound to Him. By obeying the lesser authorities we pay homage to Him.

A question readily comes to mind: How could God be related to a godless government? This is a question that is troublesome to people who wrestle with the church's responsibility in matters of civil obedience. This passage in Romans, however, is not an isolated one in the New Testament. Again and again we are told to "honor the king" and to subject ourselves to the magistrates. Peter instructs us to submit ourselves to the civil authorities so that Christ might be honored (1 Peter 2:13, 14). Two things need to be understood here. First, the biblical concept of all earthly governments is, in a sense, hierarchical. All human authority, from the dogcatcher to the governor to the senator to the president, comes under the authority of God and of His Christ. Now, does that mean that every one of these human authorities exercises godly rule? Of course not. It is very possible, as Paul speaks of it, for there to be spiritual wickedness in high places (Ephesians 6:12).

Oscar Cullmann, the Swiss theologian, suggested that governments in this world can become utterly demonic and stand in fierce opposition to the reign of Jesus Christ. Yet, the operative principle in the New Testament for the Christian is to obey the civil magistrate. This is done not to exalt the human authorities, but because we recognize that behind them stands the authority of God. A natural question to Peter's statement is: how does my obedience to the political institutions and civil authorities bring honor to Jesus?

Throughout Scripture sin is not viewed merely in an individualistic manner. The Bible sets forth a concept of corporate solidarity where there is such a thing as institutional sin. In our broad understanding of sin biblically, we see that sin is not merely individual, but that there is a complex of evil in the world.

Satan, as the prince of this world, is the one who stands behind this complex of evil. He is identified biblically as the anti-Christ, the one who exalts himself above Christ, and who moves and works contrary to the work of Christ. The word *anti* means "in place of" or "against." Both of these thoughts describe activities which we associate with the figure of the anti-Christ. He is one who stands against Christ and who seeks to take the place of Christ. The basic activity of the anti-Christ is to induce a spirit of disobedience. The Bible calls this "lawlessness." In fact, Paul, in the Thessalonian correspondence, refers to the anti-Christ in terms of his historical manifestation as the "man of lawlessness." In the end of the Sermon on the Mount, Jesus warns, "Many will say to me in that day, Lord, Lord, have we not prophesied in thy name? and in thy name have cast out devils? and in thy name done many wonderful works? And then will I profess unto them, I never knew you: depart from me, ye that work iniquity (Matthew 7:22, 23).

Lawlessness—the Essence of Sin

One of man's greatest problems is the spirit of lawlessness. That is the essence of sin. There would be no death, no murder, no wars in this world if, in fact, every person were lawful and obedient to the authority of God. The disobedient spirit of man, which began when man refused to obey God, now spills over into a natural, corrupt propensity to resist all other authority. Biblically speaking, the Christian is asked to bend over backwards to respect authority wherever he sees it. He is to exhibit a spirit of obedience rather than of lawlessness.

This attitude was manifested early in the Christian church in the face of persecutions. For example, consider the work of Justin Martyr, the first great apologist of the early church. He was aptly named because he gave his life for the faith. In the second century A.D., he wrote the first "apologia" or reply, addressing his essay to the Roman Emperor, Antoninus Pius. He attempted to answer the charges being brought against Christians. Nero could not simply throw people to the lions or use Christians as human torches without some kind of legal justification. Charges had been brought against Christians, including the charge of atheism.

Why atheism?

Because Christians did not believe in the gods of the Roman pantheon. They would not bow down and worship Jupiter.

Christians were also accused of being cannibals. It was known that they gathered together to eat someone's body and to drink his blood.

A third and most notable reason for persecuting the Christians was prompted by the charge that the Christians were seditious insurrectionists. They refused to recite the loyalty oath of the empire which, in effect, deified the emperor. This oath required them to simply say, "Caesar is Lord," but the Christians refused. Instead, they said, "Jesus is Lord!" Therefore, they were accused of civil disobedience because they refused to give absolute allegiance to the emperor. Consequently, they were thrown to the lions.

When Justin Martyr wrote to the emperor, he attempted to explain the Christian position. He said in effect, "Look at us. We are model citizens. Our religion teaches us to pray for the emperor and to be submissive. We are called to pay our taxes and to honor you. We drive our chariots within the speed limits. When it comes to the daily matters of civil obedience, we are the model citizens of your empire. However, there is a limit to what we may do. We cannot worship you."

The early church understood this emphasis in the New Testament. They were not given to anarchist activities or to revolutionary plotting. They recognized that Jesus had earlier rebuked the Zealots who were seeking to overthrow wicked governments by the power of the sword.

Should a Christian Always Obey?

Some have concluded, therefore, that Christians must never disobey civil authorities. Can we come to that conclusion biblically? Of course not. In Acts, when Peter and the apostles were commanded by the authorities to stop preaching, they replied, "We must obey God rather than men" (Acts 5:29 NIV). We can only conclude that if the civil authority commands us to do something that God has forbidden, or forbids us from doing something that God has commanded, not only *may* we disobey, but we *must* disobey! We must always obey God rather than men. This does not include disobedience simply because we do not like the policies or because they inconvenience us, or even because they cause us to suffer. God has not commanded us to live a life free of suffering. But if the civil magistrate instructs us to deny Christ, we have to disobey the civil magistrate. The basic emphasis, however, is the posture of bending over backward in order to be submissive in a spirit of humility whenever and wherever possible as long as we do not compromise our commitment to God.

A further reason for obedience to government is not only because God stands behind it, but because He ordains government in the first place. In Genesis we see that Adam's dominion over the animals is the first expression of authority on this planet. Adam was elevated to the position of prime minister over the creation. However, Adam and Eve as human beings were ruled by God. Notice that there is an authority structure built into creation, but in that original authority structure, there were no governments. There were no princes or kings in the Garden of Eden.

Only after the Fall of man was human government established. Consider the situation: as soon as Adam and Eve were expelled from Eden, they were forced to live "east of Eden." They must have had a certain degree of homesickness. It would have been nice to return. However, if they returned they would not have been able to get in because an angel was posted at the gateway to the Garden of Eden with a flaming sword. The purpose of this sword was to keep them out. The sword was an instrument of restraint, an instrument of force.

With this in mind, let us return to our most basic definition of government. Any kind of government that exists, whether it be socialistic, communistic, oligarchic, plutocratic, democratic, or monarchic, is force. It is for the protection, the sustaining, and the maintaining of human life and property. God invests governments with authority and the power to back up that authority. That is why governments not only have law, but they also have law enforcement agencies.

A few years ago a United States senator said to me, "I don't believe that any government ever has the right to coerce its citizens to do anything."

I said, "That's a noble sentiment, senator, but what I've just heard you say is that no government ever has the right to govern. If governments don't have the right of coercion, what can they do but suggest? You have law without law enforcement." I reminded him that the power of the sword was established in the Old Testament.

God gives the civil magistrate the power of force. He does not give it to the church. Remember that Jesus denounced Peter's use of the sword in the Garden of Gethsemane

(Matthew 26:52). The church does not have the power of political coercion, but the state does. The function, design, and purpose of the sword are to protect the innocent and to restrain the evildoer.

It has been said (and has now become a cliché) that power corrupts and that absolute power corrupts absolutely. If this statement were absolutely true, it would mean that God is absolutely corrupt. At face value, it is not a truism. However, when we use that statement with respect to human beings and human institutions, we recognize that the tendency of fallen man, when given a taste of power, is to aggravate, intensify, and accelerate corruption as that power increases. The more power we give a fallen man, the more likely we will see corruption. History has borne witness to that.

Is Government a "Necessary Evil"?

Some have concluded, therefore, that all governments, because they involve power, are evil. Therefore, a Christian should have nothing to do with serving in government because to do so is to invite personal corruption. The idea that government is *necessarily* evil, however, casts a shadow upon the God who has established it in the first place.

Saint Augustine once called government "a necessary evil." By that he meant that government itself is made *necessary* by the fact of evil and even though governments may be oppressive and exploitive and corrupt, the worst government is still better than no government. The "no government" idea gives absolute freedom to unrighteous people who can wield their power and corruption against the innocent and the weak who are defenseless. Pure anarchy is the law of the jungle that God abhors. God Himself stands behind world governments, using them for His ends and for His glory. He uses them primarily as instruments to restrain the power of evil. No matter how evil that government may be, things could conceivably be worse. If God removed all human restraints, our lives would become intolerable. Therefore, He has instituted government and given that government the sword of force to which we are called to righteously submit whenever possible.

God does use evil men to accomplish His purposes. There are times when I am called to submit to those evil men, not in order to sin, but to be under their authority.

Thomas Aquinas differed with Saint Augustine. He was convinced that government would have been necessary even if man had not fallen. As the world was populated, commerce would be established upon the basis of a division of labor. In this format, government would have arisen to maintain norms of weights and measures and to provide necessary benefits to the common good.

One final consideration must be addressed. What if we as Christians are called to serve in government? This includes service in the armed forces as well as work in the statehouse. If the government is doing the task that God has called it to do, there is no reason why a Christian should not be expected to participate. We must not accept the idea that the church relates to God and that the state does not. This is a crucial point. Historically, in this country we have separated the church and the state, but both church and state are under God. The church has its function to perform and the state has its function to perform. When the state is performing the function to which God has called it, we, as subjects of God, should not resist it but participate in it.

For many people, the concept of separation of church and state has come to mean the separation of state and God, as if the state ruled autonomously on the basis of its own intrinsic authority. Christians must never believe that. Instead, we must see that state as answerable to God, ordained by God, and as a legitimate vehicle for the people of God to serve God.

It is certainly legitimate, and in some cases desirable, for Christians to be actively involved in the political process. I see no reason why a Christian should not or could not run for state office and serve Christ by being a godly ruler. However, it becomes increasingly difficult for a Christian to get elected, playing the "games" that are often demanded of that person, without compromising his integrity. That is the razor's edge that a would-be Christian politician has to walk. It is still possible in this country to be elected to high office without compromising one's personal integrity. It may be difficult, but it is still possible.

If, in our vocation, we are able to serve the world by serving our fellowman in government, we are not acting against Christ. Quite the opposite is true. Government is an arena in which we as Christians are called to bear witness to the righteousness of Christ and to the style of government that Christ Himself exhibits. This does not mean that we take the church into the state. It does mean that we take Christians and their obedient life-style into government. The Christian lives in both spheres, church and state, and he has responsibilities to each. As a Christian responsibility, we are called to be subject to the powers that be.

Questions for Discussion

1. Why is government force?

2. What is meant by the phrase, "You cannot legislate morality"?

3. Should and do governments pass legislation on moral matters?

4. When should you disobey the government?

5. How do you respond to the adage, "My country, right or wrong"?

6. What is meant by separation of church and state?

7. What is justice?

8. What is the government's role and responsibility with respect to protecting and maintaining life?

9. How are economic freedom and political freedom related?

10. Can a Christian participate in war?

Index

property, 146–148; equity, 147–149; industry,
147–149; compassion, 146–150.
Dynamics of: production, 148, 150–152, 154; tools, 151,
152, 154; capital, 152, 154; profit, 152–155; division of
labor, 154, 155, 208
Eichmann, Karl Adolph, 94, 95
Einstein, Albert, 117
Empiricism, scientific (*see* Logical positivism)
Enlightenment, the, 64, 79, 98
Epicureanism, 131–133, 137
Erasmus of Rotterdam, 63, 64
Eve, 159, 205, 206
Evolution, 99, 108, 115–117, 160, 163
Existentialism, 26, 30, 32, 41, 70, 101; definition of, 42–46;
pessimistic variety of, 46–56; contrasted with Christian-
ity, 56, 57; synthesized with Christian values, 58, 59

Faithism, 109
Fellini, Federico, 51, 129
Fideism, 109
Freedom, existential, 55, 56

Galileo, 160, 161, 166, 167
God: sovereignty of, 24, 62, 117, 145, 146, 198, 202, 207;
transcendence of, 35, 36, 98, 114, 187; eternalness of,
36, 105, 163
Government: and state-imposed religion, 23, 72; as problem solver, 79, 88–90; and economic regulation, 88,
90–94, 155, 156; bibilical view of, 197–209
Graduated income tax, 48, 87
Gresham's Law, 91, 92

Hedonism, 26; origins of, 129–133; contrasted with Christianity, 134, 137, 138; and drug/alcohol addiction,
135–137; and the sexual revolution, 136, 137
Hedonistic paradox, 131